I. Berry, William A. (William Aylor), 1915--
I. Alexander, James Edwin, 1930--

The paper in this book meets the guidelines for permancence and durability of the Committee on Production Guidelines for Book Longevity of the Council on Library Resources, Inc.

1 2 3 4 5 6 7 8 9 10

JUSTICE FOR SALE

The Shocking Scandal of
The Oklahoma Supreme Court

William A. Berry
James Edwin Alexander

Macedon Publishing Co. : Oklahoma City

Contents

Illustrations

DEDICATION

Carolyn Berry

Preface

"He may be a son of a bitch but he's *my* son of a bitch, and that makes a difference." That comment came from a prominent lawyer regarding a certain public official, regarding whom there had been stories, rumors and innuendoes about his participation in activities that resulted in a huge financial windfall--so much so it raised questions about his ethics in office.

That little episode, innocuous though it may seem, typifies an all-too-common attitude toward public officials. People tend to forgive, forget, overlook, or be indifferent towards actions that are not only morally wrong but also against the law. This attitude has enabled many politicians to remain in office long after they should have been removed. People tend to be forgiving of their friends so long as they themselves have not been victimized.

Huey Long remarked if he had "ten good friends" he could be elected to any office in Louisiana. The help of these friends does not come cheaply. It carries expectations to reciprocate. The newly-elected officeholder begins to feel, *He helped put me into office, and if he needs a favor I'm going to help him if I can.* The person asking the favor seldom has the best interests of the officeholder in mind. He is usually pursuing his own self-serving ends. Failing to deliver on behalf of one's "friends" often carries heavy penalties, chief of which is defeat in the next election.

Several of my friends have asked why I am writing this story of judicial corruption now. They acknowledge that the events chronicled here form a part of Oklahoma's history, but they would prefer to see the whole sad, sorry episode remain covered from public view. "What good can come of it?" some asked.

This book is written, in part, because I was an eyewitness to the prosecutions. As a member of the court, I experienced the repercussions that resulted from the political corruption of a few judges. I played a modest role in bringing about the prosecutions, a contribution that was not disclosed at the time. Now, thirty years after the fact, there is little benefit that can come to me from making my participation known.

A second reason for telling this story is so the citizens of Oklahoma may have a greater understanding of how corruption can occur in high places and why it is so necessary to maintain their vigilance. Eternal vigilance has always been the price of freedom. Continued vigilance is necessary because the forces of corruption are wide and have many tentacles to reach deep into the most sacrosanct of offices.

A third reason for telling the story is more mundane and practical. Throughout the period of the supreme court scandals, my secretary and I collected the newspaper articles and bound them into a large scrapbook. It grew to more than 3,000 clippings in all. I never gave up on the idea of finding some means whereby the people of Oklahoma could have access to this material in one place where it could be easily read and understood.

Dr. James Alexander, who collaborated with me on an earlier book, *Prisoner of the Rising Sun,* reviewed the clippings and offered his opinion that the material was worthy of publication and could be formed into a book. This is the result of that effort.

Whatever else may be said, this *is* Oklahoma history. It may not be the most savory kind of history, but it is *our* history. Is there a lesson from it? Only time will tell. But as for me, I was there, I was caught up in the circumstances, and I reacted the only way I felt I could act as a true guardian of the law.

William A. Berry, January 1996

1

Call to Justice

I had barely walked in the door of my home after a full day at the Oklahoma Supreme Court when my wife, Carolyn, said, "Bill, you're wanted on the phone." She handed me the receiver.

"Judge Berry, this is Stephen Chandler. Can you come over to my house right away? I want to talk with you." It sounded urgent.

The year was 1965. The day was Tuesday, January 12. The time was 5:45 p.m. Stephen Chandler was the federal judge presiding over the Western District of Oklahoma.

I remember the date well because it was exactly six years earlier, January 12, 1959 when I was sworn in as a justice on the Oklahoma Supreme Court. That was the proudest day of my life.

For the life of me I could not imagine what Judge Chandler wanted to talk to me about, or why it was so urgent he couldn't have called me at my office. Almost certainly, it didn't have anything to do with any case currently before the court. The federal and state courts were two separate judicial systems, and the two sets of judges did not often interact on the cases before them.

On the other hand, my acquaintance with Chandler dated back several years, though our relationship had never ripened into what one would call a truly personal friendship. For one thing, there was a disparity in our ages--Chandler was about 20 years my senior. His nephew, Morgan W. Cox, had married into my wife's family and sometimes Chandler and I saw each other at family gatherings, but even then we didn't have much in common to talk about. Then too, when I was Assistant U.S. Attorney--this was back in the 1947-50 era--I tried cases in Chandler's court from time to time. But apart from these rather tenuous ties, I was not able to think of any special reason why Chandler should be calling me at this time in the afternoon on such an urgent note.

Nevertheless, I felt the matter must be a serious one. It didn't occur to me to ask what the matter was about; I simply put my hat and coat back on and told Carolyn where I was going. ''Dear, that was an important call and I have to step out for a few minutes. I shouldn't be gone long.''

Carolyn trusted me implicitly and didn't ask where I was going. She was a lovely brown-eyed blonde whose grandfather was the legendary G. A. Nichols, founder of Nichols Hills and developer of Lincoln Terrace and several other early-day Oklahoma City residential areas. She and I met in 1945 at the naval hospital in Norman, Oklahoma where I was recuperating from ailments incurred as a prisoner of the Japanese in the Philippines during World War II. She was a Red Cross volunteer. We married the following year.

Climbing back into my still-warm car, I drove through the chill January dusk from my home on Wilshire Boulevard over to Judge Chandler's house on Grand Avenue, a distance of less than a dozen blocks. Chandler was nervously waiting for me at the door when I arrived and he quickly ushered me inside.

Known for maintaining a secluded, almost reclusive, life style, Chandler seemed to be living in perpetual fear for his life. Typical of his precautionary nature was the way he took personal telephone calls. Whenever someone wanted to call him at his home, the caller would first have to route the call through Vera Howard, his court clerk at the U.S. District Court. She was the only person who knew his home phone number. Vera, for her part, would dial the judge's private number, wait for the phone to ring a predetermined number of times, then hang up. Immediately she would dial the number again. That was the signal for him to pick up the phone. Vera would relay the message and Chandler would then call the person back.

Stephen Chandler was a tall, very distinguished gentleman somewhere around 65 years of age, thinning white hair, rugged build. His wife had been dead for many years. He had a personable quality about him that could make you feel as if you were the most important person in the world. At the same time, however, there were a lot of lawyers who wanted him off the bench because he tended to run the court with a firm hand.

Chandler hurriedly closed the door behind us and bolted it with a series of security locks. As he did so, the thought ran through my mind, *This is almost like going into Fort Knox.*

"I have to be very careful," Chandler explained somewhat apologetically. "I don't know when someone might try to take advantage of my situation. I know it sounds neurotic, but I even have to watch my water for fear someone might seek to put poison into it."

I found myself thinking, *I don't know exactly what he is expecting to happen, but it certainly seems as if he is very anxious about something.*

We were still standing awkwardly in the entryway, and I was waiting to be invited on into the house. But the rest of the house appeared to be dark. "Have a seat," Chandler offered, motioning towards a settee against the wall. He took my topcoat and hung it on the hall tree, then drew a chair up close so that we sat face to face.

"I want to show you something," he said, nervously thrusting out a sheaf of papers. I quickly glanced down at the packet. It appeared to contain a sworn statement of some sort.

"This is Judge Corn's confession," Chandler explained. "It was taken by former county attorney James Harrod and U.S. Attorney Andrew Potter when they went up to visit Judge Corn in his cell at the Federal Penitentiary at Springfield, Missouri. I want you to read it."

The person he was referring to, of course, was 80-year-old

Judge N. S. Corn, a supernumerary justice of the Oklahoma Supreme Court who, in July of the previous year, had pled *nolo contendere* (''no defense'') to a charge of income tax evasion and was sentenced to 18 months in federal prison. At the time Corn's sworn statement was taken, he was serving out his sentence at the medical center for federal prisoners at Springfield, Missouri. On December 19th, however, he had been released after having served less than five of the eighteen months. Corn's early release from federal prison created a minor stir in the press and led some people to speculate as to what kind of deal he may have cut in exchange for gaining his freedom.

The statement Chandler handed to me told a sordid, sickening tale of bribery and collusion on the state's highest court. It made me feel sick to my stomach just to read it. In his statement, Corn recounted the details of receiving bribes in connection with two cases before the supreme court--*Selected Investments Corp. v. Oklahoma Tax Commission* and *Marshall v. Amos*. In the *Selected Investments* case, Corn reported that Hugh Carroll, then head of Selected Investment Corp., had made a deal to pay the sum of $150,000 for a favorable opinion in a legal dispute over state taxes. Out of this $150,000, Corn paid $7,500 to Justice Earl Welch and $7,500 to Justice N. B. Johnson to secure their votes in this case, and kept the rest for himself.

Judge Corn also told of having received $4,000 from an attorney for a reversal in the *Marshall v. Amos* case. According to his statement, Corn had a long-standing agreement with said attorney to vote as the ''sixth man'' in all cases in which that attorney was involved. The term ''sixth man'' was new to me, and I wasn't sure exactly what was meant by it. Nevertheless, I read on.

When I got to the last page, I observed that the document bore the signature of N. S. Corn, notarized and dated December 9, 1964. Obviously, it was authentic.

I let the document drop onto my lap. I stared off into space, scarcely allowing myself to believe the damning words of my former colleague. Described here were the actions of three justices, impugning the integrity of the whole court, and violating the very canons of truth and fairness.

Judge Chandler waited for me to digest the disgusting information, then he looked at me intently and asked forcefully, "Now that you have read it, what are you going to do about it?"

For a long moment I remained silent, then I answered him in somber tones, "Judge, I don't know what to do with it."

"Well, can't you figure out something?"

"Judge, I don't know yet what I will do, but I promise you that I will *do* something." That was as much as I could promise at the moment.

Chandler advised me that I could take the statement with me; however, he made me promise not to let anyone else see it without his permission. "My giving this document to you may be improper," he said, "but I feel strongly that justice needs to be done. I don't have any other way to see that justice gets done."

"But isn't this something the county attorney should handle?" I protested.

"The county attorney, Jim Harrod, has been sitting on this statement for over a month now, and he hasn't done a thing about it. I think he's glad to now be out of office so he doesn't have to deal with such a hot potato. I have every indication that his successor, Curtis Harris, plans to do nothing either. As a result, I'm deathly afraid the whole issue will just get swept under the rug."

"Then why don't *you* be the one to do something?"

"I can't. My hands are tied. The federal court does not have original jurisdiction here. There is a rule that prohibits federal courts from intervening in the state courts unless specifically authorized by Congress. Accordingly, this is a matter that will have to be handled at the state level, and that is the reason I am putting it in your hands."

"But why me?"

"I have thought about that hard and long. It boils down to this, you're the only one I can trust. You know, there are some people out there who want to sweep this scandal under the rug because they don't want to bring shame on the court. In addition, you've got some powerful legislators out there who want to squelch any court cleanup because they like things the way they are.''

With that admonition, we said our goodbyes. I drove back home in the gathering darkness, visibly shaken by what I had seen and heard.

2

Shaking the Foundations

Naturally, I had been aware of the *Selected Investments* case even before Judge Chandler handed me the documents. It had dominated the newspapers for months. Furthermore, I was fully conscious of the fact that two of my fellow justices had been convicted of income tax evasion. Indeed, my celebrated walkout on Justice Welch had garnered front-page coverage. The only thing I didn't know until now was the depth and scope of the deceit.

Driving homeward that dark and gloomy January night, my mind couldn't help reflecting back on the series of events that led up to this sorry situation. The illegal activities began to unfold seven years earlier--before I was elected to the supreme court.

At that point in time, the conspirators sought to blame it on "Pierre Laval." He was the fictitious, mysterious French-Canadian oil promoter whose creation opened a Pandora's box and unleashed a torrent of woes.

The fictional Laval was a creature of the tangled web woven by Selected Investments Corp., an Oklahoma investment management company founded in 1929 with Hugh Carroll as its president. By the mid 1950s, the company had gotten into financial and regulatory trouble; early in 1958 it was declared bankrupt.

Attorney Luther Bohanon was appointed to represent two of the receivers.[1] Bohanon commissioned an audit of the firm's financial records that showed $200,000 had been withdrawn from Selected Investment's trust account by Hugh Carroll. Ten days after the withdrawal the Supreme Court of Oklahoma handed down a decision in the case of *Selected Investments Corp. v. Oklahoma Tax Commission* wherein the supreme court overturned a lower court decision unfavorable to Selected Investments and granted them a judgment in the amount of $500,000.

Carroll testified that he had withdrawn the money to buy oil properties in Canada. He stated that he had given the funds to a French-Canadian named Pierre Laval, who had subsequently absconded with the money. Carroll said that he did not know if Laval was living or dead and that he felt as though he had "just bought the Brooklyn Bridge."

Justice Earl Welch, then chief justice, authored the opinion which reversed the suit in favor of Selected. Vice Chief Justice N. S. Corn was the second to sign the majority opinion, followed by Justices Denver Davidson, N. B. Johnson, Ben T. Williams, and W. A. Carlisle. A dissenting opinion was written by Justice Floyd Jackson and concurred in by Justice W. H. Blackbird.

The bankruptcy proceedings led to criminal charges being filed against Hugh Carroll and other officers in his corporation. On October 22, 1958, Carroll, his wife Julia, and three associates were indicted by a federal grand jury in Oklahoma City on 31 counts of mail fraud and conspiracy. They were subsequently convicted and sentenced.

On sentencing Carroll, Judge Ross Rizley commented, "I don't know what you did with that money. I don't think you have it. But I don't think you turned it over to Pierre Laval."[2]

Meanwhile, the IRS was quietly conducting its own investigation. Nothing more was heard of the case, or of "Pierre Laval", for another three years.

Then, on Monday, April 6, 1964, the dike burst. A federal grand jury was called into session in Oklahoma City. In an unusual move, the U.S. Supreme Court itself specially charged the grand jury. The in-state federal judges felt that it would be inappropriate for any of them to try a state supreme court judge. Following existing procedures, they requested that the U.S. Supreme Court appoint a judge from another circuit. Federal Judge Roy W. Harper of the 8th Circuit, St. Louis, was assigned by the U.S. high court to preside over the hearings.

The first witness to testify was Hugh Carroll. He was followed by Linwood O. Neal, trustee of Selected's $39 million trust fund. On the second day, prominent Oklahoma City attorney O. A. Cargill appeared. He, in turn, was followed by Oklahoma Supreme Court Justice Earl Welch. Next, Welch's former wife, Mrs. Fern Welch appeared and gave secret testimony, and also Welch's sister-in-law, Mrs. Ophia Taylor.

On Wednesday, April 8th, Justice Welch was back on the stand for several more hours--making more than eight hours overall that the judge had spent before the federal grand jury. Late that same afternoon, the grand jury announced two indictments that sent shock waves throughout the Oklahoma citizenry. The announcement came too late in the day to make the evening newspaper, but the next day's banner headline of the *Oklahoma City Times* trumpeted the news:

"TWO JUSTICES POST BOND ON TAX EVASION CHARGES"

"Welch and Corn Put Up $5,000; State Probe Due"

"Noncommittal and outwardly calm, two state supreme court judges made bond Thursday on federal income tax evasion indictments.

"Justice Earl Welch avoided most newsmen and photographers by walking into U.S. Commissioner William C. Page's office about 8 a.m. to sign a $5,000 appearance bond and then going into the county jail to be photographed and fingerprinted.... Supernumerary judge N. S. Corn came in at the scheduled hour and ran into reporters and photographers waiting at the commissioner's office.

"The two men were indicted on five counts each by the federal grand jury late Wednesday. Welch, 72, is accused of evading federal income taxes from 1957-1961. Corn, 80, is charged with evading taxes from 1957-1961, and making an untrue tax return for 1958 and 1959."[3]

The two men had been colleagues on the court for more than 30 years--Welch came to the bench in 1932 and Corn just a year later in 1933.

Salary for supreme court justices for the years in question was $12,500. However the government published a table charging that the two judges' taxable income (net of all deductions) exceeded their salary by a considerable margin during some of those years.

Justice Corn was arraigned before Judge Harper on April 23. Through his attorney, James R. Eagleton, Corn sought to plead "no defense." On Wednesday, July 1, Harper accepted Corn's "no defense" plea, but only after the government read into the record a statement of the evidence on which the indictment was based.

U.S. Attorney B. Andrew Potter, flanked by two tax attorneys from the Justice Department, charged that the government had evidence that $150,000, most of it in $100 bills, was paid to Corn after the supreme court reversed a lower court decision in 1957. He also charged that Corn told a witness that the money would go to "assist himself and other members of the supreme court in meeting campaign expenses." Although no names were mentioned by Potter, his statement fit the facts in the old *Selected Investments Corp.* case and recalled the mysterious Pierre Laval. The government showed that Corn reported only about 40 percent of his correct taxable income for the years 1957 and1958, resulting in an understatement of income of $11,063.54.

Reporters from the *Oklahoma City Times* were on the scene to cover the proceedings: "Nelson S. Corn, 80-year-old retired justice of the state supreme court, was sentenced Wednesday to 18 months in federal prison and fined $11,250 for income tax evasion.

"The sentence was imposed by U.S. District Judge Roy W. Harper, St. Louis, shortly after the supernumerary judge changed a previous plea of innocent to one of "no defense" to a 5-count grand jury indictment.

"Tall, somewhat stooped and hard of hearing, the retired veteran of 24 years' service on the high court...who retired in January, 1959...showed little outward emotion after the sentencing.

"Judge Harper said he was aware of Corn's age and the fact that he has paid the tax owed plus the penalty. But he added, 'If the only penalty for tax evasion was payment of the fine, in my judgment many, many more persons would take the chance because so few are investigated.'

"He observed, 'I realize that incarceration won't help this defendant...but we live in a country where we must have law and order and we must have deterrent to things like this'."[4]

Corn's attorney appealed to the court for lenience because of his client's advanced age and poor health. Harper replied that the only defendants he has not sent to prison in tax matters are those who are not physically able. He said he wouldn't be satisfied with statements by the defendant's own doctor; Corn would have to be examined by government doctors or doctors acceptable to the Justice Department--or at Corn's expense, by other doctors agreeable to the government.

Both sides agreed that 30 days would be enough time to complete the medical examination. In the meantime, Corn was allowed to remain free on bond.

Reaction among the legal community was as swift as it was forceful. Shocked justices of the Oklahoma Supreme Court convened for a conference later that day and called for the immediate resignation of Corn as a supernumerary judge.

Chief Justice W. H. Blackbird made the call to Corn at his home. As related by *Daily Oklahoman* reporter, Ray Parr, Blackbird said, "I told him I thought it would be in the best interest of the court if he would submit his resignation at this time. I believe it is in the best interest of the bar and the courts of this state that he resign at this time."[5] Corn's response was to say that "he would think about it and suggested he would let us know in a few days or a week or so.''

When asked what might happen if Justice Corn refused to resign, Blackbird acknowledged, ''I don't know what the court will do if he doesn't resign.'' He went on to explain that the law creating supernumerary judges makes them subject to impeachment by the legislature the same as members of the supreme court. ''No other means of removal from office is provided,'' he said. To make matters even more awkward, the legislature could act only when it was in session.

I was approached by the reporters for a comment. The *Oklahoman* quoted me as saying that the claim by U.S. Attorney Potter that a witness had said Corn was paid $150,000 in return for a favorable ruling in a pending case came as a ''shock'' to the court.

''I would like for him to say who the others were,'' I told them. ''It's not fair to other members of the court.''[6]

Governor Henry Bellmon called for a vigorous investigation by state agencies into what he called ''a sickening and despicable corruption in the highest judicial court of our state.'' The governor announced the appointment of his attorney, Dale Cook, to coordinate between various agencies evaluating the question of bribery. ''It is clear that direct and positive action by the appropriate agencies of this state must be coordinated to vigorously investigate and pursue this matter to a final conclusion,'' Bellmon said.

Jim Standard, writing for the *Daily Oklahoman,* interviewed me on how this issue might affect the chances of passing a judicial reform package. I said to him, ''The federal charges may 'enhance' the possibility of passage of a judicial reform measure that will be on the ballot in November. That measure, called the 'Missouri plan', is designed to take judges out of politics.''[7]

Judge Welch's turn at the bar of justice came Monday, October 5, 1964 when the bailiff called to order the federal court on the second floor of the federal post office building in Muskogee, Oklahoma. Judge Harper opened the trial of the *United States v. Earl Welch.* Welch was accused of evading $13,364.74 in taxes for the years 1957 through 1961.

Welch's attorney was V. P. Crowe, head of one of the leading law firms in Oklahoma City. Crowe was very familiar to me. As a matter of fact, he and I had played golf together a few times--I think he shot in the high 90s. He was very personable, very likable, small in stature with a very thin build.

Crowe was familiar with the charges of corruption on the high court. He and I had traveled together to a bar conference in Boiling Springs, and along the way the conversation drifted to the corruption issue. Although Crowe didn't say it in so many words, he definitely left me with the impression that he didn't think the members of the supreme court were above being influenced. He certainly led me to believe that the court *could* be influenced and he knew that certain lawyers were used in that connection.

Crowe approached me about being a character witness for Judge Welch. I told him, "Yes, I will be a character witness, but I will tell the truth; and I will not tell anything but the truth so far as I see it." It was obvious to Crowe that I would be a reluctant witness. He never called me.

Opening statements to the jury began on Tuesday, October 6. Government attorney, Don Hansen, an assistant in the Department of Justice, Washington, D.C. said witnesses and evidence will show that Justice Welch had an unreported income of $40,000 to $50,000 during the five years which comprised the five counts of the tax evasion indictment against him. Hansen told the jury that Welch could not have saved $53,000 (an amount he placed in a safe deposit box) from the time he started practicing law in Antlers from 1911 to 1932 when elected to the supreme court.[8]

Welch's chief attorney, V. P. Crowe, reserved his opening statement until later.

When testimony began on Tuesday morning, it became clear the case was going to rest on showing that Justice Welch spent more money than he declared on his tax returns. A half-dozen witnesses were called to the stand in an effort to show where the judge spent his money.

Testimony was enlivened by the judge's former wife, Mrs. Fern Welch, who was on the witness stand for an hour and twenty minutes. The 72-year-old justice, who had previously displayed no emotion during the trial, visibly clasped and unclasped his hands while she was on the stand.

Mrs. Welch, who married Welch in 1917 and divorced him in December 1958, painted a picture of him as a very frugal man during their long marriage. Under direct examination, Hansen asked if he had "money outside of his bank account."

"Not that I know about," she replied.

"Did he have a safety deposit box in Antlers?

"Yes."

"Did he keep any money in it?"

"I don't know."

Hansen then paused. "Prior to the 1958 separation, was Judge Welch going with another woman?"

Welch's attorney leapt to his feet and shouted objections. Judge Harper ordered that the jury leave the room and then held a conference with the attorneys.

Hansen declared, "The government proposes to show that Judge Welch was going with another woman prior to the divorce and that he spent money on this other woman." Crowe objected that the question was designed to prejudice the jury.

Judge Harper ruled that the court was not interested in whether Welch was going with another woman, but if he spent money on her it was proper to be disclosed at trial. The jury was called back and admonished to ignore the question.

Hansen rephrased his question, "Prior to the separation was Welch spending money on another woman?"

"I discussed the woman with him (Welch) but not about spending money," she replied.[9]

Testimony from witnesses on Wednesday attempted to show that Welch played a role in the purchase of a home in 1953 for the woman who later was to become his wife. W. J. Strawbridge testified that Welch was present at the closing of an August 4, 1953 sale of a house to Mr. and Mrs. W. F. Taylor and Ruby Myers. It later developed that Mrs. Taylor was Ruby Myers's sister and the house was subsequently transferred to Mrs. Myers. It also developed that Mrs. Myers married Judge Welch shortly after he was divorced in December 1958.

Fireworks popped on Wednesday when Mrs. Ophia Taylor, sister of Ruby Myers, took the stand. Mrs. Taylor suddenly seemed to suffer a loss of memory when asked a series of questions about when and how long she had been acquainted with Welch. Again and again she pleaded, "I don't know," or "I don't remember."

Judge Harper lectured her on the penalties of perjury.

Mrs. Taylor, now on the verge of weeping, admitted paying bills for her sister, before her marriage to Welch, at an exclusive dress shop. She used $100 bills to make the payments.

The next day's witness list brought the credit manager of Balliet's, an exclusive women's dress shop in Oklahoma City. She testified that over a 27-month period, a total of $3,300 of the present Mrs. Welch's account was paid in $100 bills. Apparently in an attempt to show that the present Mrs. Welch had no source of income except for that provided by the judge, Hansen introduced into the record a statement from the IRS that the former Mrs. Myers--whom other witness have said was never employed--had no record of paying an individual income tax from 1945 through 1958, the year she and Justice Welch were married.[10]

The courtroom was packed at 2:12 p.m. Friday for the appearance of former supreme court justice N. S. Corn. Now in failing health and nearly deaf, Corn was driven by automobile that morning from the federal medical facility at Springfield, Missouri, where he was serving 18 months for tax evasion.

Corn was assisted to the witness stand by federal marshals and his attorney Richard Fowler. A hospital technician stood nearby. His shirt was open at the neck and he wore no necktie. Two sons, Lonnie and Burton Corn, both of Bartlesville, Oklahoma, were among the spectators.

After cursory questions, Hansen asked, "Do you know Judge Welch?"

The former justice replied: "Let me state at this time, claiming my privilege under the Fifth Amendment on advice of counsel, I decline to answer the question for the reason the answer might tend to incriminate me."[11]

For another sixteen times, Corn gave the same answer to sixteen other questions. At length, a frustrated Hansen told Judge Harper, "I think it is fruitless to try to examine him further."

Throughout Corn's appearance, Welch leaned forward in his chair and listened intently.

The second week of testimony began with another big name witness, Hugh Carroll, now free from a two year prison term for fraud. The jury was not permitted to hear Carroll's testimony. Welch's attorney argued that the testimony was not competent or admissible.

Sending the jury out of the courtroom, Harper conducted a preliminary hearing as to Carroll's testimony. Speaking clearly and matter-of-factly, Carroll told of paying $150,000 to Judge Corn in return for the reversal of a lower court ruling against his corporation. He said he gave Corn $25,000 as a good faith deposit, and the other $125,000 after the decision had been handed down.

Asked directly, "Who is Pierre Laval?" Carroll replied, "I don't know, and that was a fictitious story."[12]

At last, the six-year-old mystery of "Pierre Laval" was solved! Hugh Carroll acknowledged that he had simply made the story up when pressed for an explanation as to what he had done with the missing $150,000 from Selected's trust fund.

On Wednesday, October 14, the government closed its case. After nine days of testimony, the issue boiled down to one major factor: did Welch have $56,599 in cash squirreled away at the beginning of 1957? The government claimed he did not.

Principal witness for the defense was Lee R. Christenson, a

certified public accountant from Oklahoma City. Christenson traced Welch's financial history from 1911 until December 31, 1956 in an attempt to establish the defense's contention that the high court judge had $56,500 in cash on January 1, 1957, the beginning of the prosecution years.

Christenson was back on the stand Friday for four hours of intense cross-examination by government attorneys. Hansen hammered away at the accountant. "This witness admitted he had never asked Welch about this cash and the witness said he used only statements in preparing his charge from information supplied only by Welch," Hansen said.

Justice Welch did not take the stand to defend himself. "We are ready to rest," his attorney announced.

The case went to the jury at 3:45 p.m. Precisely one hour and 47 minutes later the jury returned with a verdict. Justice Earl Welch was convicted on all five counts of evading federal taxes.

Daily Oklahoman reporter Katherine Hatch was there. "The 72-year-old veteran state supreme court justice remained impassive, scarcely blinking as the verdict was read by jury foreman S. E. Loy, Jr., Muskogee businessman," she wrote. "Except for the sound of Loy's voice as he read the guilty verdicts, the courtroom was silent until the session ended."[13]

Judge Harper deferred sentencing until November 13.

Despite being convicted of federal tax evasion, Welch remained a full-fledged member of the Oklahoma Supreme Court. The state's constitution had no provision to remove a justice of the supreme court except by impeachment by the state legislature. The next regular session of the legislature would not convene again until January 5, 1965.

That improbable situation drew a plea from Governor Bellmon for Oklahomans to create a "supercourt" that would have the same power as the legislature to remove judges. "The conviction of Judge Welch yesterday points up an obvious need in Oklahoma for a method of assuring that our judiciary not be allowed to become corrupt," he said. He urged voters to approve a constitutional amendment which would create a court of the judiciary with the power to retire or remove a judge for just cause.

Voicing the opposite view was House Speaker J. D. McCarty, who said it was too early to talk about house plans for an impeachment charge against Welch. "I don't know what we'll do until the session meets," he told reporters, adding, "Perhaps by that time the full record will be written."[14]

On November 13, Welch was given a sentence of three years imprisonment and a $13,500 fine. His attorneys appealed to the U.S. Court of Appeals, but that appeal was denied. Eight days later, the U.S. Supreme Court refused to review Welch's conviction. That cleared the way for him to begin serving his sentence, now set to start February 14, 1965.

For many people, now wearied of hearing of court scandals, appeals and convictions, there was a strong current of sentiment for wishing the problem would just go away. "All this has given the state's high court a black eye, but it's about over now," groused one citizen.

If the people of Oklahoma were under any illusion that the matter was going to die down soon, they were in for a rude awakening.

The Oklahoma Supreme Court began its new term on Monday, January 4, 1965. The justices gathered in the conference room for what was called "work basket" day, the time we normally handled motions and other routine matters concerning the court's activities.

Much to my surprise and chagrin, Justice Earl Welch entered the room. He said. "I don't think I had better attend the conference, but I will tell you how you can dispose of cases where you won't need my vote."

His effrontery irritated me completely. Here was a convicted felon awaiting the start of his sentence and he was trying to tell the court how it should conduct its business.

I stood up and announced, "If the Chief Justice please, I am going to leave the conference room if Judge Welch is going to tell us how to conduct our business and dispose of our cases.''

Welch's face turned red. He reared back in his seat and snarled, ''Look here, I don't appreciate you talking to me that way, and I want you to take it back!''

''Judge Welch,'' I said to him, ''I'll take it back, but it's not going to change one thing. I am still going to walk out of this conference room!'' With that, I stormed out.

Charging down the hallway, I passed *Times* reporter Hugh Hall. Sensing something was amiss, Hall caught up with me and asked, ''What's the matter with you? Why did you walk out of the conference room?''

''I have no comment at this time except that I asked to be excused,'' I said. Then I added, ''But get Judge Blackbird in an interview. Perhaps he will tell you.''

Smelling a story, Hall cornered Blackbird and got the story he was looking for.

Page 1 headlines in the afternoon paper screamed: ''IT'S A BERRY BOYCOTT.''

Hall wrote, ''A member of Oklahoma's supreme court stalked from the court's private chambers Monday morning when convicted Justice Earl Welch sought to present a matter to the seven other justices.'' Hall went on to say that I had told Chief Justice Blackbird that I would not remain in conference if Judge Welch tried to participate while under conviction of federal income tax evasion charges.[15]

The next morning's editions of the *Daily Oklahoman* and the *Oklahoma City Journal* also headlined their versions of the same story.

The attention of the press now focused on the supreme court, watching its every move. It was increasingly obvious that the problem was not going to go away. Something more forceful would have to be done.

Maybe that's why Judge Chandler called me. My celebrated walkout persuaded him I *would* do something.

3

Shattering the Icons

Upon returning home from my fateful meeting with Judge Chandler, I closeted myself upstairs for the entire evening while I mulled over the implications of the burden he had placed on me and its ramifications. It seemed a dark cloud was hanging over the state's supreme court--*my court!* Not only over the court, but over the whole system of case law. If judgments could be influenced by bribes, then all the carefully constructed pyramid of legal precedent might begin to crumble.

How do you restore the honesty and integrity of the court? I asked myself. *How do I work with some judges who are dishonest when the rest are honest?*

There was no doubt in my mind but that the information needed to be made public and the guilty parties brought to justice, whoever they might be. But I wondered how in the world I should come out with the information. The county attorney, Jim Harrod, had the information; why did he just sit on it? What about Curtis Harris, his successor, why didn't he jump in the middle of it? Was there some political reason why they just stood there looking at each other? There were some powerful names mentioned in the report: were Harrod and Harris afraid of putting their lives or political careers in jeopardy by making this information public? If this were so, would I be putting my own career on the line?

The more I thought it over, the more it made sense to me that however this information was to be made public, it needed to be done by someone who could claim a cloak of legal immunity, particularly since the document named some very powerful individuals. My next question was, who possessed such a cloak of immunity?

Some people might argue that as a justice of the supreme court, I would be immune from legal reprisal. Perhaps this was what Stephen Chandler had in mind when he gave it to me. However, I didn't see it that way. Three obstacles stood out in my mind. In the first place, Corn's sworn statement had been conveyed to me personally and was not legally before the high court, in which case I would be acting as a private citizen if I released the information, not as an officer of the court. Moreover, since some of the people named were very high-powered lawyers, and knowing that they could bring suits against me very easily if they had a mind to, I naturally hoped to avoid being hog-tied with an endless series of libel suits. Indeed, I had often quipped, "You don't need grounds to file a lawsuit, you only need a lawyer."

In the second place, among the names mentioned in Corn's confession were some of my fellow justices currently serving on the court; if my name were tied to the report's release, that could create a certain amount of awkwardness on the court. And in the third place, I also had to consider the fact that I was a Democrat while the governor of the state was a Republican. If things got politicized and the legislature turned against me, I could not count on having the benefit of a strong ally in the governor's office to come to my aid.

The governor was Henry Bellmon, ex-Marine and farmer from Billings, Oklahoma, who had come into office in 1963 as the state's first Republican governor. I was not well acquainted with Bellmon personally, but I had positive feelings towards him. He was a solidly built man, about six feet tall, dark hair, who looked somewhat out of place on those rare occasions when he had to don a tuxedo. Public speaking was difficult for him--he was noted for the three-by-five cards which he turned in his hand and referred to as he spoke. But public speaking wasn't everything.

He made a good governor. Bellmon's strong suit was his reputation for honesty and integrity; if any money was made in politics during his regime, he wasn't a part of it.

Bellmon was a down-to-earth guy, not at all pretentious. One time he invited all the judges from both the supreme court and the criminal court of appeals to the mansion for dinner. We were seated at card tables set up all over the mansion. The governor and his wife, Shirley, helped to serve the meal and clear the dishes--just as if we were at Sunday dinner at a friend's house.

I knew I could count on his integrity, but I didn't know if I could count on him politically.

After having enumerated the reasons why I felt I should keep myself in the background, my attention turned next to thinking about *who* would be the ideal person to carry the message to the public. The obvious answer, in my mind, was that it should be a member of the state legislature. Why? Because members of the legislature are automatically granted legislative immunity for any statements they make on the floor during a legislative session; and fortuitously, the legislature was currently in session.

Having decided to ask a legislator to put out the information, my next question was, *which* legislator? My first impulse was to call on my good friend, Nathan S. "Nate" Sherman, Democrat from Oklahoma City. Sherman was highly regarded for his integrity and held the position of majority whip in the House of Representatives.

Conceivably, a more logical choice might have been House Speaker J. D. McCarty. However, I didn't know McCarty as well as I did Sherman. Besides I had reason to believe, based on some of his prior pronouncements, that McCarty might try to block its release. Therefore, since Nate Sherman was a respected member of the leadership structure, he would certainly have the opportunity--if he were willing--to gain the floor on a matter of personal privilege.

Having made that decision, I was then able to go to sleep. Carolyn didn't ask what was troubling me and I didn't volunteer any information. I didn't want to cause her worry.

Just as soon as I got to my office the next morning, I placed a call to Judge Chandler down at the federal courthouse to lay out my plans. He readily agreed to my idea of asking Nate Sherman.

But my attempts to reach Sherman came up empty. The representative was not in his office, so I left a message for him to call me back. I did not hear anything. All the next day and again on Friday, I left messages for him. Still no return calls.

Becoming progressively discouraged by the lack of a response from Nate Sherman, I started thinking in another direction. *Who else in the legislature can I turn this over to?* I asked myself. This line of thinking led me to consider someone from the other side of the political aisle.

G. T. Blankenship was the Republican minority leader of the House of Representatives. He and I had developed a friendship stemming back several years when I had delivered some lectures at the University of Oklahoma Law School while he was still a student there.

Before contacting Blankenship, however, I got back in touch with Judge Chandler and told him there would have to be a change in plans. Chandler indicated that he knew Blankenship and said he thought he would be a good man for the job.

That Sunday afternoon, I telephoned Blankenship and told him, "I have something that I think would be of great interest to you. Can you come over to my house?"

Blankenship said, "Sure," and he immediately drove over. About thirteen years younger than me, G. T. Blankenship was about my height--nearly six feet tall, had a ruddy complexion, light reddish-brown hair, and bore himself with an almost military-like posture. In the words of one compatriot, he was a "man on the go."

At the time I telephoned, my in-laws were at the house visiting. The children, Nick and Libby, were upstairs playing. When Blankenship arrived, I excused myself from our company and led him into my study and closed the door behind us. "G. T.," I said, handing him Judge Corn's confession, "you have to read this!"

Blankenship read through the document. "Where did you get this?" he asked incredulously.

I said that Judge Chandler had the document in his possession. I recounted the circumstances under which Chandler had conveyed it to me.

"This is awful!" Blankenship exclaimed. "How could something like this go on right under our noses and we not know about it?"

I said, "Well, G. T., ever since I can remember, there have been rumors and jokes circulating about justice being bought and paid for at the court. As a matter of fact, my family was involved in a case a few years back in which we felt the other side paid someone off. Judge Corn's statement happens to be the first really concrete admission that there may be some truth to those rumors."

"I still find it hard to believe," he replied.

I outlined my strategy of enlisting someone who bore the cloak of legislative immunity who would agree to make the information public. Then I asked him point blank, "G. T., would you be willing to read this from the floor of the House of Representatives and take it up as a matter of personal privilege?"

Unhesitatingly, Blankenship said yes. Still clutching the document, he asked, "May I take this with me?"

"I'm not allowed to give you the actual document, and I'm not really sure legally you even *want* to be in possession of it," I replied. "But I can let you copy whatever portions of it you think you might need."

For the next half hour or so, Blankenship wrote out on a yellow legal pad those parts of Corn's confession that he planned to read to the legislature. Except for substituting the name "Mr. X" in place of the powerful lawyer who had carried Judge Corn on his payroll to vote as the "sixth man," he made no other changes in the text.

"G. T.," I said, placing my hand warmly on his shoulder as he left, "this takes a tremendous amount of courage on your part."

He nodded agreement, weighed down by the knowledge that he

was about to touch off a firestorm in the legislature, the likes of which Oklahoma had never seen before. Where it would lead, and where it would end, neither of us could possibly know.

When Blankenship got back to his home that Sunday afternoon he took his wife, Libby, into his confidence. G. T. first swore her to secrecy, then he filled her in on all the details. Over the years, he found she could be trusted to maintain confidentiality. He told her that Judge Chandler and I were involved.

Libby Blankenship expressed vehement opposition to her husband's involvement. "You don't know what these people will do to you," she said. She ticked off a long list of objections.

G. T. replied, "I know, but one of the reasons you run for public office is to perform a service that needs to be accomplished."

Nevertheless, after voicing her protestations, Libby agreed to stand by her husband in whatever actions he felt were necessary for him to take and said she would follow him wherever the consequences might lead.

The 36-year-old lawyer-politician's career was on the line: if successful, here was a vehicle that could launch him into higher office, and if he failed he might never practice law in Oklahoma again.

The Republican party didn't have much political power in Oklahoma. At the time Blankenship was elected to the state legislature in 1960, voter registration in the state was 5-to-2 Democrats over Republicans. Indeed, he was the first Republican since 1928 to be elected to the legislature from Oklahoma County.

Therefore, Corn's sworn statement--wielded wisely and well--could become a powerful weapon for bringing about change, not only on the supreme court but in the legislature as well. Blankenship viewed this as a marvelous opportunity to do some good.

Public outcry for an investigation into the high court, which had begun as soon as Judge Corn had pleaded "no defense" back in

July, went nowhere. Governor Henry Bellmon, for his part, called for a vigorous investigation into the question of bribery. "The citizens of Oklahoma are entitled to know the full facts and whether other members of the court are involved," Bellmon declared.[1]

Leaping on the bandwagon was Oklahoma County Attorney Jim Harrod, who pledged that he would make available to the grand jury--scheduled to convene September 4--all information he had concerning the alleged bribery of supreme court justices.

Also leaping into the fray was U.S. District Attorney B. Andrew Potter, who told the federal court he had a witness who would say that he paid $150,000 to Justice Corn. Corn, Potter charged, told the witness the money would help pay the campaign expenses of some of the other court justices.[2]

Despite these pious pronouncements, however, the various investigative efforts fizzled and eventually came to nought.

Again in October, the hue and cry was taken up anew when Justice Welch received his conviction. Governor Bellmon, attending a political rally in Pawnee, stated, "I am seriously considering calling a special session of the legislature for the purpose of considering impeachment proceedings against Judge Welch, unless he chooses to resign from the court immediately."[3]

On the other side was House Speaker J. D. McCarty. Speaking against such a move, he said it was too early to talk about house plans for an impeachment charge against Welch. McCarty pointed out that Welch's conviction would be appealed, and until a final order is written in the case there is always the possibility the conviction could be reversed.[4]

Not content to leave reform to the legislature, the Oklahoma Bar Association created a new and embarrassing problem for Earl Welch. In an open letter published in the *Oklahoma Bar Journal*, October 31, bar president James D. Fellers wrote: "The Rules Creating, Controlling and Regulating the Oklahoma Bar Association, provide that upon receipt of a certified copy of the record of conviction of a member of the Association of a felony, the Court shall suspend such member until the time for appeal has elapsed or the judgment of conviction has been affirmed on appeal at which time the Court shall order such member disbarred."[5] He placed the matter on the agenda of the Executive Council on November 12.

The big question at this point was, could the bar association sanction a judge? The supreme court in a 14-year-old case had already held that judges are not subject to disciplinary action by the bar. However, as Fellers explained, the action proposed by the bar was intended to deal with Welch as a lawyer--not as a judge.

The state supreme court answered that question on December 10th by taking away Welch's right to practice law. The order, however, did not affect his status as a member of the court. In a heated dissenting opinion, Justice Ben T. Williams assailed the order as a "vain, purposeless, useless and futile act, an idle gesture."[6]

In his dissent, Justice Williams wrote: "The people of Oklahoma suspended Judge Welch from the active practice of law when they elected him to become a member of this court in January, 1963. He may not practice law while he remains a member of this court."

Williams continued, "Not one member of the public could be harmed by his practicing law. That is because he cannot lawfully practice law while he remains a judge of this court. To my mind, no question of morals is properly involved in this proceeding."[7]

Welch himself, through his attorney, issued a bitter statement. "I do not know how they could have done this," Welch said. "I cannot see why they would, but of course they are upset and disturbed by the adverse publicity and the jury verdict. This order is such a vain and useless move. It does not change a thing."[8]

Meanwhile, over at the legislature another battle was brewing. House judiciary committee chairman, Rep. John McCune, a Tulsa attorney, was beating the drums for impeachment. McCune was in the process of preparing a brief which outlined the legal procedures necessary to impeach the 73-year-old judge. In a nutshell, the procedure called for the house to bring charges and the senate--which sits as a judge--to convict. It was widely expected that impeachment proceedings would begin early in the session when the legislature convened again on January 5.

J. D. McCarty, whom the newspapers accused of "hemming and hawing" or of "foot-dragging," seemed exceedingly reluctant to allow the house to take up the impeachment trial of Welch. The *Enid Morning News* complained, "At one time the speaker said he wasn't sure whether tax evasion was an impeachable offense and then he had other excuses for not acting."

In a move that was widely perceived to be a device for heading off the judiciary committee, McCarty created a brand new committee to delve into the matter. He gave this new committee--the Committee on Research and Investigation--precedence over the already existing judiciary committee. The speaker named Rep. Lou Allard, a newspaperman from Drumright, as chairman and saw to it that Allard's committee was staffed with people who were within his own inner circle of power.

Tensions were building as January 5th drew closer--and with it, the opening of the 1965 legislative session. McCune's committee on the judiciary seemed intent on bringing a resolution to force the impeachment issue. McCarty, on the other hand, in the words of *Times* investigative reporter Jim Standard, "asked McCune not to introduce an impeachment resolution on the first day of the session so it would not conflict with opening day ceremonies."[9]

On Wednesday, January 6, Rep. John McCune introduced his resolution, HR 505, which called for "an investigation into the acts of Earl Welch, justice of the supreme court of Oklahoma, for the purpose of determining whether or not Articles of Impeachment be preferred against him." In support of his resolution, McCune said, "There is a misconception among some people that Welch must be presumed innocent until his appeal has been decided," McCune said. "However, Welch no longer should be presumed innocent. He was guilty from the moment that jury came back with a verdict of guilty. Today, Earl Welch stands guilty of a felony."[10] McCune's resolution charged that Welch's conviction amounted to "moral turpitude" and "corruption" in office.[11]

Speaker McCarty routed the resolution to the rules and procedures committee, which he controlled. There was no discussion. The speaker acknowledged to reporters that the Welch case was being referred to the rules committee to delay action on it. "This is being done to slow the matter down for a few legislative days until we can get organized," he said. "We do not want this disturbing the organization of the house."[12]

Many people knowledgeable in the ways of the legislature viewed McCarty's move as a way to bottle it up. Indeed, the following week the rules committee, meeting in closed session, duly voted 16 to 3 against proceeding with the impeachment move. When asked how he felt about it personally, Speaker McCarty shed a little light on his own motivations in the matter when he said that "some lawyers feel evasion of income taxes is not an impeachable offense."[13]

Regarding the Welch trial itself, the speaker alluded to the government's case as a cock-and-bull theory. All that the government proved, he said, was "the net worth theory."

The *Tulsa Tribune* found the legislature's lack of curiosity to be dismaying. The editor wrote, "We've seen legislative committees throw tantrums because minor state employees have padded expense accounts with a few drinks or used state cars to haul their children to school. Those tribulations of our time will not diminish if the legislature repeats such investigations but permits the big ones to go untouched. Indeed, the public will either laugh the bold hunters out of office if they go after mice with shotguns but drop their weapons and run every time bigger game appears, or we'll head into a situation where everything goes, and the bigger it is, the smoother it can operate."[14]

In answer to reporters' questions, the speaker stated that another meeting of the rules committee was slated for Thursday, January 21, at which meeting he would invite Welch's attorney, V. P. Crowe, to attend. McCarty listed four alternatives that the committee could recommend. The committee could decide if it wants to hold up the resolution for a while longer. Or, it could decide to pass the resolution on to the house research investigation committee (1) without a recommendation, (2) with a recommendation that the committee hold up for a while, or (3) proceed with it at once.[15]

"Some members have some very definite and strong ideas that this should not be rushed into because of all the implications involved," McCarty said.[16]

That was it. To cynical observers, it now appeared as if the matter had all the makings of another legislative whitewash. House leadership had effectively sealed off all avenues of access. That is to say, if the resolution never came out of the rules committee, legislators would never have an opportunity to vote on the merits of impeachment. Procedure had triumphed over substance.

Thursday, January 21, dawned overcast and cold in Oklahoma City. The outside temperature was 37 degrees. Oklahoma City newspapers were filled with stories about President Lyndon Johnson's inauguration the day before, and about former British Prime Minister Winston Churchill, who lay dying in England.

Times reporter Jim Standard profiled J. D. McCarty whose picture, incidentally, bore a remarkable resemblance to Ralph Cramden, the character portrayed by comedian Jackie Gleason in *The Honeymooners* television series. The story was headlined, "'King' J. D.'s Own Program Is Clicking."

Standard wrote: "The big round man in the state capitol corridor let loose a resounding horse laugh, followed by an exaggerated wink of his right eye.

'What sales tax resolution?' he bellowed. 'Has there been anything introduced on the sales tax?'

"J. D. McCarty knew his good-natured deception would not be taken seriously.

"By then, only hours after two freshmen house members introduced the measure calling for a vote of the people on a one-cent sales tax increase, it had become apparent McCarty had made his move to take over the 1965 session of the legislature.

"Not that anyone suspected for a moment he wouldn't.

"Generally conceded to be the strongest man in state government, McCarty was a cinch to take control and head the house in writing a program for Oklahoma....

"McCarty's power in the house has led to speculation he will enter the 1966 governor's race. Many of his friends insist this will be his last term in the house of representatives.

"The house speaker admits he is thinking about the governor's race."

Standard closed his piece with the observation, "Whatever program Oklahoma receives the next two years, chances are good it will be the handiwork of the big round man."[17]

The Oklahoma State Legislature was gaveled to order at 11:00 a.m. on January 21 in what was thought would be a short, uneventful session. The normal schedule was to meet in afternoon sessions on Mondays, Tuesdays and Wednesdays, and on Thursdays the lawmakers would meet in the morning, adjourn about noon, and go to their home districts over the weekend.

G. T. Blankenship was nervous--scared, actually. As a matter of fact, before going into the chamber that morning, he took the precaution of informing his close friend Tom Taggart what was about to happen. Taggart was a fellow Republican member who was elected to the house at the same time as Blankenship in 1960. "Tom," Blankenship told him, "I want you to know what's going to happen this morning, so if I don't ever leave that chamber, at least somebody will know what this is all about."

Actually, Blankenship didn't really believe that physical harm would come to him on the floor of the chamber that morning, but he was worried about what might happen to him afterward. Some of the most powerful names in Oklahoma were involved and their entire lives were at stake as far as their reputations and careers were concerned. Blankenship had no way of knowing what their reaction might be, but he felt strongly that someone might get hurt before this was all over.

Following the roll call, there was the introduction of several new bills, a second reading and referral of other bills, and standing committee reports from Agriculture, Revenue and Taxation, and Judiciary.

The rules committee reported that it had again delayed a decision on whether to proceed with impeachment proceedings against Judge Welch. Clearly, the pressure was heavy to halt the proceedings. During its meeting, the committee: (1) agreed to reach a decision the following Tuesday, (2) authored and sent to the house a resolution calling for a vote of the people at the next special election to set up a court on the judiciary, (3) heard Rep. John McCune urge that Welch be impeached or suspended from office, and (4) heard V. P. Crowe urge that no action be taken until all of Welch's appeal rights had been exhausted.

Blankenship rose and asked for the floor on a matter of personal privilege. Having been recognized, he began reading from a written text.

"Mr. Speaker, ladies and gentlemen of the house. What I am about to say should be cause for the great concern of us all. I speak to you in a triple capacity. First, as a member of this responsible body; second, as a member of the bar of this great state; and last and most important as a citizen.

"I felt it necessary to speak out, for to me, next to a house of worship, the most sacred public institution is and must be a court room. The very basis for the success of our form of government has been the unique and eminently successful separation of powers into the executive, legislative and judicial. The latter having separate and equal powers and responsibilities with the former. The honorable members of this honored profession are entitled to have the tarnish removed. More important still, the confidence of the citizenry as a whole, in their court system, is as important as the human rights produced by that same system.

"On December 9, 1964, at Springfield, Missouri, former Justice N. S. Corn made a sworn statement. This statement was sworn to before an officer authorized to administer oaths as well as in the presence of a then county attorney from Oklahoma and a U.S. attorney from Oklahoma. This document reveals a story so sordid, sickening and discouraging, its contents must be revealed for the good of us all. Corn relates as having been involved in an agreement with a certain lawyer since prior to 1940. This agreement was simply to vote with the majority as the 'sixth man' in all cases in which the lawyer was involved. For this service, Corn was given several thousand dollars.

"In 1956 this same lawyer agreed to pay Corn $4,000 for a reversal in *Marshall v. Amos.*

"Also in 1956, Hugh Carroll agreed to pay Corn $150,000 in the *Selected Investments Corp. v. Oklahoma Tax Commission* case. 'I got Judge Welch, Judge Johnson and Mr. X to help,' Corn swore. The 'Mr. X' is a fictitious name supplied by me. 'After the opinion became final, Hugh paid me $150,000, I paid Welch $7,500, Judge Johnson $7,500,' Corn says.

"He tells of receiving $25,000 from Carroll in cash by having it placed in the glove compartment. Also of receiving the other $125,000 ten days or so later.

"He relates a sad but reprehensible picture of not believing his own ears at the amount so he wrote it down for the next meeting in order to confirm the large figure. He tells of meeting with Judge Welch in Welch's office, and, I quote, 'What was said in that conversation, Judge? Well, I just told him I had been acquainted with Hugh Carroll for a long time and Hugh Carroll's mother and stepfather lived there at Taloga, and I thought the deal was all right. I thought we could depend on it. I didn't think anything could slip.' 'You didn't tell him, though, how much you were getting?' 'No, No. I just told him that there was $7,500 for him if he could go along on the opinion.'

"He tells of a similar conversation with Judge Johnson in Johnson's office. He was asked, 'Do you recall when you paid that $7,500 to Judge Welch in that Selected case?' 'Yes, it was the same afternoon I got the $2,500. I came right back to my office...' 'Q: The $25,000?' 'Yes, the $25,000. When I got the $25,000, I came back to my office and I counted out another $7,500, put a rubber band around it, and delivered one package to Judge Welch in his office and one to Judge Johnson.'

"He relates that a certain lawyer lost only one case before the court in his entire tenure of 24 years. I could go on and on but it wouldn't accomplish anything. I have read the document. I have considered its contents carefully. I certainly do not know of the truthfulness of Corn's statements. I do know that the statements were made. That fact alone is sufficient to incur the attention of this body. The peoples' faith is shaken. It is the duty of the legislative branch to show them the difference between an unworthy individual and an unworthy court. The honest, faithful members of the court must be vindicated. An investigation by an arm of this body can, properly pursued, restore the confidence of the people and clear the innocent. I have a resolution on the table, Mr. Speaker."[18]

Blankenship's resolution, HR 512, called for the judiciary committee "to investigate and study the matters herein" and to "submit its final report and recommendations" within sixty days. The speaker referred the resolution to the Rules and Procedures Committee.

Speaker McCarty seemed visibly shaken. Democratic house members began screaming "shady politics." Rep. C. M. Spearman, Jr., Democrat, Edmond, asked Blankenship where he saw the alleged statement by Corn.

"I am not at liberty to say," Blankenship answered.

Spearman replied, "It appears someone is playing politics."

Following a tumultuous adjournment, the outcry spilled out into the corridors and hallways outside the house chamber where Spearman and other Democrats continued their criticism. Spearman said it was no coincidence that a member of the minority party had been able to obtain Corn's statement. "I went to the U.S. attorney's office myself and tried to get documents on the case," Spearman, a lawyer, said. "I was not able to, and I don't know how Blankenship got it."[19]

Democrats were complaining the move was made in an effort "to make it look like the Democrats aren't doing anything on this."

"I feel as if I had just been shafted," J. D. McCarty remarked off the record.

Mary Jo Nelson, writing the story for the *Times*, concluded with this observation: "Blankenship's move to get the Welch impeachment proposal put into the hands of the house judiciary committee was interpreted by some as showing discontent with the handling of the case by the rules committee."[20]

Naturally, everybody wanted to know who the mysterious "Mr. X" was. But Blankenship refused to say. His strategy was *one enemy at a time*. That is, he wanted to keep the attention focused on the supreme court issue and he reasoned that if he introduced the name of someone not on the court, then--tantalizing though it might be--the whole matter might get diffused. *Besides*, he thought, *it will add a little drama to it.*

Blankenship had not anticipated the furor and the outcry his statement had engendered. He had an appointment to meet after the close of the session with a fellow law school alumnus, a lawyer from Amarillo, Texas, who was visiting in Oklahoma City. But the continuing discussion and debate on the hill made it difficult for him to break away.

When Blankenship finally did arrive at the motel where his friend was staying, the friend proudly held up a copy of the early afternoon edition of the *Oklahoma City Times* emblazoned with banner headlines: "3 JUSTICES LINKED TO BRIBERY CLAIM." Not only that, the *Times* carried the lawmaker's picture above the masthead. Blankenship was absolutely floored to discover his speech had that kind of immediate response or that a newspaper could respond that quickly.

Friday morning's *Daily Oklahoman* concurred with Mary Jo Nelson's opinion. Reporter Otis Sullivant wrote, "Rep. G. T. Blankenship, Republican minority leader, has forced a full-scale house committee investigation of alleged bribery of two justices of the state supreme court."[21]

The article hints that the rules committee was deliberately suppressing an investigation into the court scandal. It praised Blankenship for having taken "the bold step in speaking before the house of representatives to make the information available to the public and news media. He got it out in the open for consideration, discussion, investigation and clarification.''

As to whether McCarty and the rules committee could any longer keep the matter bottled up, the *Oklahoman* article opined, ''Legislative leaders conceded that the rules committee will have to authorize a full-scale investigation or the house and its leaders will come in for a great deal of public criticism.''[22]

Finally, recognizing the courage shown by Blankenship, the article concluded with this thought: ''Blankenship, as an attorney, ran a risk to his reputation as a member of the bar and legislature, by bringing the statement of Corn into the open, but it should end the reluctance to have the investigating committee go into the matter.''[23]

In politics, timing is everything. Blankenship's statement could not possibly have come at a more propitious moment. The press had been chipping away for months at the delaying tactics employed by J. D. McCarty and his house cronies. The media had accused him of ''hemming and hawing,'' ''foot-dragging,'' and showing extreme reluctance to launch an investigation. Until then they didn't have anything really solid to go on.

Coming, as it did, only minutes after a rules committee ploy to ''kill'' the investigation, Blankenship's public pronouncement threw the issue into sharp contrast. The facts of the scandal were now out on the table for everyone to see. The issue was seized by the press and from now on the public--not McCarty--would control the agenda.

In a word, the genie was out of the bottle.

The morning after, Chief Justice Blackbird called a judicial conference. The high court justices all trooped in and sat in their accustomed places. Justice Johnson was a little late in coming in. When he sat down, he put his head down, shook it, and said, ''Oh, I don't understand, I don't understand.'' He shook his head again and said, ''Oh, that son of a bitch. That son of a bitch.''

No one asked him who the "son of a bitch" was--whether he meant G. T. Blankenship for standing before the legislature, or Justice Corn for giving the information to the prosecutors, or someone else.

Justice Blackbird reported that James Fellers, president of the Oklahoma Bar Association, called to see if the bar association could be of any help in investigating this matter. He said the bar's Board of Governors wanted to meet with us to help work through the crisis we were in. Blackbird then opened the matter for discussion.

I spoke first. It was the custom of the court for the junior member to lead off. "Yes, I think it is a wonderful thing that the state bar association has come to our aid, because certainly we are all in this mess," I said. "We have all been tarred by the same brush, we all stand accused."

The meeting took place in the bar association building on Lincoln Boulevard, just south of the state capitol. We were all seated around the conference table and each of the justices was asked to stand and tell what he thought ought to be done to resolve the crisis.

I began by thanking the Board of Governors for their interest, saying we were appreciative of the fact that they were coming in on the problem. "We are in a situation where we can't defend ourselves," I said. "It's a lot like the old saying, 'A lawyer who has himself for a client has a poor lawyer'."

At one point, I made a suggestion: "In the interest of openness, all members of the supreme court should offer their signed income tax returns for the previous year--and any other years they might choose to--so that the bar association could check to see just where the money was, if any, and if there had been any money received by the justices."

No one objected at the time, but when the meeting was over, Judge Welch--who also attended the meeting--told me that turning over our income tax statements wasn't a very good idea. "We are sticking our necks out to the legal profession," he said. "I don't think it is any of their business.''

Chief Justice Blackbird designated me to be the one who should meet with the press in representing the court to the public. He didn't offer any explanation for the assignment, but I surmised that he felt that since I was not on the court at the time the alleged activities took place, I was thereby free from taint. Also, I suspected that maybe he didn't want to be pestered by a persistent press asking embarrassing questions such as, ''How could you let these things go on under your nose?''

Governor Bellmon called for G. T. Blankenship to come into his office. The governor said he wanted the Oklahoma State Bureau of Investigation to run a ''sweep'' on Blankenship's home telephone, as they had information that it might very well be bugged. Blankenship gave his okay.

Bellmon went on to warn him, ''I don't know what your habits are, or who you hang out with, or what you do; but my advice is that at the close of the session every day until this matter is over, go home. Don't go any place where you might be compromised, either fairly or unfairly. But just look after yourself, and don't give the people involved any opportunity.''

Although the governor didn't name names, he strongly intimated the party was going to get rough and some of the players were going to get bruised before it was over.

4

The House Investigates

Speaker J. D. McCarty found himself in a box. Now that Blankenship had revealed startling information on the floor of the house chamber, McCarty had little choice but to allow the investigation to go ahead. To impede the investigation further would raise too much of a stink.

McCarty's major problem now was how to keep his own image from being tarnished while, at the same time, positioning himself to run for the governorship in the next year's election. The scope of the investigation had expanded to include not only Justice Welch but also Justice N. B. Johnson, whom McCune had not named in his original resolution. Up until the time Blankenship revealed the contents of Corn's sworn statement, there had been nothing on the public record that linked Johnson to the scandal.

Speaker McCarty was not the only one embarrassed by this turn of events. County attorney Curtis P. Harris, who all along had in his possession a copy of Corn's statement but failed to act on it, was particularly incensed. He launched a broadside attack against Blankenship. "It appears to me Mr. Blankenship has a copy of some statement," Harris railed. "My only criticism is that if he wants to read it on the floor of the house he should quit being a yellow belly and name the so-called Mr. X which is alluded to time and again."[1] Covering his backside, Harris averred Blankenship did not obtain the statement from him.

Governor Bellmon was quick to come to Blankenship's

defense. The governor called on Harris to make any information he had available to a legislative committee investigating the supreme court. "This needs all the light possible," the governor said. "It needs to be cleared up, not covered up." Bellmon said anyone who attempts to interfere in the legislative investigation is "damaging the confidence of the people of Oklahoma in the judiciary."[2]

Harris's "yellow belly" statement, the governor added, made Blankenship's motives "look partisan...which they were not."[3]

On Tuesday, February 16, another storm was unleashed at the federal courthouse. Newspaper headlines proclaimed, "CARGILL INDICTED ON 3 PERJURY COUNTS."[4] The previous day, after only four hours of deliberation, prominent Oklahoma City attorney O. A. Cargill, Sr., was indicted on three counts of perjury by the same jury which had indicted former justices Corn and Welch on income tax evasion charges. The jury indicted Cargill for "willfully and knowingly" lying in his testimony April 7, 1964.

Cargill, 79-year-old former Oklahoma City mayor and one-time county attorney, denied any wrongdoing. "I am positively and emphatically not guilty of this unwarranted indictment," he said.[5]

Blasting an unnamed witness who allegedly testified against him, Cargill said, "Our grand jury system has stooped to a new low when a self-confessed ex-convict who harbors a bitter dislike for someone can dip his slimy tongue into the cesspool of perjury and procure an indictment against an innocent man, then, I say, 'God save this nation from some form of tyranny'."[6]

He also denied offering a bribe to justices or putting undue pressure on them to influence court rulings. Cargill would not give out the name of the "ex-convict" he referred to in his statement.

The first count of the indictment charged that Cargill had paid bribes to "a member or members" of the state's highest court and was closely involved in the *Selected Investments Corp.* case. Cargill had testified under oath the previous April that he did not know what had happened to the $150,000 paid to Justice Corn.

The indictment alleged that Cargill "had conversations both with Hugh Carroll and Corn, Oklahoma Supreme Court justice, concerning the payment of $150,000 by Carroll to Corn to obtain a favorable ruling in the case of *Selected Investments Corp. v. Oklahoma Tax Commission,* decided by the supreme court in 1957...and Cargill had in fact received a portion of the aforesaid sum of money."

The second count concerned "Pierre Laval," the fictitious French-Canadian oil producer named by Carroll as the recipient of the $150,000. In his April 1964 testimony, Cargill said he didn't know who Pierre Laval was and that he had never heard of him until Carroll told about him in a court trial. The grand jury charged that Cargill "knew Pierre Laval was in fact a fictitious person; that he was in fact familiar with the story recited by Hugh Carroll from the witness stand prior to having heard same in said courtroom and did in fact know more about said story than merely that he heard it in said courtroom, inasmuch as he (Cargill) while giving counsel to Carroll, had created and originated the Pierre Laval story as so testified to by Carroll."

The third count alleged Cargill had previously lied with regard to "on a number of occasions" having paid certain amounts of money to a member or members of the supreme court "to obtain favorable rulings." The indictment charged, "Furthermore, Cargill had a general agreement with one supreme court justice covering a period of approximately 20 years, whereby Cargill was to see to it that said justice received not less than $1,000 each time said justice ran for re-election, and said justice in turn agreed in certain instances to vote in favor of cases in which Cargill was interested."[7]

After being fingerprinted at the Oklahoma County jail, Cargill was released on $5,000 bond.

Tuesday's *Oklahoma Journal* unleashed a renewed torrent of speculation. "IS O. A. CARGILL 'MR. X'?" the paper asked in banner headlines. Reporter Daniel Webster surmised, "No official revelation has linked Cargill with the shadowy 'Mr. X' accused recently in a house speech by Rep. G. T. Blankenship of bribing high court justices. But the indictment handed down Monday by the grand jury showed a marked similarity to charges made by the representative."[8]

Blankenship refused to play the reporter's game. Still refusing to identify the mysterious "Mr. X," he said the identity of "Mr. X" was a proper subject for the legislative committee and its chairman to announce.[9]

Of more immediate concern to U.S. Attorney Potter was the possibility of "pre-trial revelations" coming out of the legislature's probe which might hamper the government's case. Potter said a legislative public hearing, in which the government's key witness might be called, would serve only to furnish the defense with a copy of testimony before a trial even takes place. Potter said that he had conferred with committee chairman Rep. Lou Allard and legal aide Rep. Burke Mordy to discuss how the legislature could proceed with its investigation without hampering the government's case. "I advised them of my viewpoint," Potter said.[10]

Not everyone agreed with Potter. An editorial in the *Oklahoma City Times* stated: "Probably this makes sense in terms of persons other than Welch possibly involved in the case. But we can't see how it is any valid excuse for the house to defer impeachment proceedings to take Welch off the bench and stop the $16,500 annual salary he is drawing at taxpayers' expense." The editorial concluded, "Otherwise we would be putting the federal interest in prosecuting a lawyer who is not a public official ahead of the interests of the state and the people's right to have an unblemished judicial department."[11]

Potter asked for an early trial date, hopefully by April 1, so that he could wind up the government's case before the legislative investigation took testimony from some of the government's witnesses. But it was not to be. Cargill successfully argued for a delay.

By late February, the House Research and Investigation Committee was ready to begin its public hearings into the bribery charges against justices Welch and Johnson. Most of the earlier meetings took place behind closed doors as the members wrangled over formulating policy issues.

Only two witnesses were heard during the closed phase of the investigation. They were Rep. G. T. Blankenship and Garrett Logan, a Tulsa attorney, who was chairman of a state bar association committee also probing the high court. Both men testified behind closed doors.

Blankenship was again given an opportunity to identify his source for the Corn document, but again he declined to do so. His source remained a mystery.

Logan presented the committee with an 84-page unsigned statement purportedly made by Justice N. S. Corn. This statement was presumed to be the same statement taken December 9 and 15 by federal and state officers at Springfield shortly before Corn's release from prison.

The investigation took a new twist when it was disclosed that three members of the house committee secretly made a weekend trip to Dallas to confer with disbarred attorney Harlan Grimes. Grimes was kicked out of the Oklahoma bar after charging that some supreme court justices and Oklahoma City attorney O. A. Cargill, Sr., had participated in a bribe in connection with the 1956 *Marshall v. Amos* case. Chairman Allard confirmed the trip when confronted by newsmen with travel claims filed by house members.

In his petition in federal court, Grimes had called Cargill the "chief briber and fixer" of the supreme court. At the time, Federal Judge Ross Rizley termed Grimes' charges "scurrilous" and dismissed the suit. Following his rebuke and disbarment, Grimes moved out of the state.

I was called as the leadoff witness on February 24. I told the committee I had no personal knowledge of bribes to members of the court.

Under questioning, I also testified that I did not know of any undue influence on members of the court. Nevertheless, I did offer the hint that some happenings seemed to ''border'' on pressure.

''What appears as pressure may be only an impression or conjecture,'' I testified, ''and I don't think this committee is interested in suspicion or conjecture.''[12] The committee did not press me to elaborate.

Asked if I had received campaign contributions from O. A. Cargill, Sr., now facing perjury charges in federal court, my response drew laughter. ''He was against me!''

Question: ''Had Cargill's son ever contributed to your campaign?''

''He was against me, too,'' I said. ''As a matter of fact, after the election, I heard that the only member of that family who voted for me was Mrs. Cargill.''

The questioner mentioned several other names. I said I could recall no contributions from any of them. As for Ned Looney, I said, ''He was very much against me.''

I reported to the committee that my 1958 campaign cost about $15,000, of which $10,000 came from my own pocket. I also provided the committee with all my financial statements and all income tax returns since I had been on the court.

However, I hedged a bit in answering questions about whether I had noticed any particular lawyers unduly influencing members of the court. ''It is difficult to know what lawyers say when they go into the chambers of another judge,'' I told them.

''Have attorneys attempted to discuss with you the merits of pending legislation?''

''I have had that happen,'' I affirmed. ''I have told them they can't do it.''

''Do any gross incidents stand out in your mind?''

''No.''

Also, I assured them that no other member of the court had ever unduly tried to influence me on any decision before the court.

Tuesday, March 2, brought Justice W. H. Blackbird to the witness table. Blackbird was chief justice the preceding two years, now succeeded on normal rotation by Justice Harry L. S. Halley.

Blackbird rocked the investigating committee when he disclosed that Justice Earl Welch was still writing opinions for the state supreme court; and, further, he had been doing so ever since his conviction. He testified that he personally had assigned 15-20 cases to Welch after the latter was indicted by the grand jury.

Blackbird sought to explain that Welch was merely handed opinions to be written, but they were approved by other justices. Welch's name never appeared on any of the opinions.

As soon as the hearing adjourned, reporters rushed over to Chief Justice Halley's office. He acknowledged that he was still assigning cases to Welch's office to research and write. "We are treating them just like supernumerary opinions," Halley explained. "I understand they are being written here at the office."[13]

My office was deluged with reporters.. Knowing that I had recently walked out of a conference with Welch, they wanted my reaction. I told them I was certainly surprised by the news, if true.

In response to questions from the reporters, I said, "I wasn't aware of that. I knew certainly that certain cases had been worked on in Welch's office, I was not aware of what he contributed. I really thought the work was more on the part of his legal assistant. In discussing the cases, I talked to his legal assistant."[14]

In his 90-minute appearance before the committee, Justice Blackbird averred he had no personal knowledge of bribes being paid to members of the supreme court. However, he acknowledged that Harlan Grimes had alleged to him that former justice Tom Gibson--whom Blackbird ran against in 1953--had distributed $20,000 of bribe money in connection with a case involving the Oklahoma City school system. Blackbird said he had no opinion as to the validity of Grimes' charges. "I knew Tom Gibson, and I knew him to be an honest man," Blackbird said.[15]

Blackbird said he did not use the information against Gibson during the campaign, but he brought it to the attention of the court after the election. He said the court declined to investigate the matter.

Justice Denver Davison was the next member of the court to be quizzed. When asked if he could think of any cases where "undue interest" was shown by other justices, Davison could only think of two. One was the *Meadors* will, in which the court switched itself on the case several times. He said that the late Justice Ben Arnold and Justice Corn were the two he had in mind. The other was the *Selected* case, in which he concurred. He said, "I thought the opinion was right and I still do."[16]

Meanwhile, a third storm was brewing at the county courthouse. The Oklahoma County grand jury had come back into session and was investigating further charges of bribes taken by the trio of high court justices.

On Monday, February 22, members of the grand jury were told they would be laying the groundwork for a far-reaching investigation of the state's supreme court over the past 25 years. In a surprise move, the jury issued subpoenas for 13 persons, including former justice Corn, to testify.

County Attorney Harris walked into the grand jury room carrying a 6-inch-thick volume of what appeared to be a shorthand reporter's transcript of testimony. When the jury recessed, Harris announced the subpoenas.

Others subpoenaed to testify included Hugh Carroll, former president of Selected Investments Corp.; Joseph Hill, accountant, who was ordered to bring all the records, books, documents pertaining to O. A. Cargill, Sr., and the law firm of Cargill and Cargill; R. O. Ingle, attorney for the Oklahoma Tax Commission and former legal assistant for supreme court Justice Johnson; and Wayne Bayless, Oklahoma City attorney, member of the state supreme court from 1930 to 1948.

An indication of how far the grand jury intended to go was demonstrated by subpoenas issued to Harlan Grimes, losing attorney in the *Marshall v. Amos* case, along with a number of persons closely associated with that litigation.

It looked as if Grimes might be getting his long-awaited day in court. Grimes had charged that a bribe of $25,000 was paid to certain supreme court members by Cargill. In a pamphlet circulated by Grimes, he alleged that he had won the case in district court in Cleveland County but the case was reversed by the supreme court. He further alleged a $20,000 bribe was paid in 1940 in another case appealed to the high court. Grimes was disbarred from the practice of law in Oklahoma May 8, 1960, by the high court on recommendation of the bar association. The bar charged that he had "both verbally and by circulation of a pamphlet alleged secret bribes were paid to members of the state supreme court for favorable decisions."[17]

The reach of the grand jury expanded. Two former legislators and a former county attorney appeared Tuesday, March 2. Max Cook, former state senator from Clinton, and James C. Nance, veteran of 34 years in the senate and house, were called for brief testimony. Cook told reporters his only connection with the supreme court other than the normal practice as a lawyer was in an unsuccessful race against Justice Floyd Jackson about 14 years earlier. Nance, a Purcell newspaper publisher, offered no explanation.

James H. Harrod, whose term as county attorney ended December 31, was called. He, along with U.S. Attorney Potter, had taken Justice Corn's statement at Springfield.

Also called before the grand jury that day was Morris Flynn, my legal assistant. Flynn had previously worked for Corn from 1937 to 1940 and from 1947 until the latter resigned in 1957.

By the nature of the case, public information on the progress of the grand jury investigation remained very sketchy. Testimony was taken behind closed doors where no reporters or observers were allowed. Witnesses were forbidden to talk with reporters. Consequently, press reports were limited to identifying the various witnesses who were called and speculating as to their testimony.

The house probe continued to dominate the headlines. On Wednesday, March 3, the committee learned about a 17-year-old affidavit that concerned a claim by O. A. Cargill, Sr., that he had the state supreme court and a district judge "fixed". The committee was told that the affidavit had been on file with the state supreme court since 1948 and the court had done nothing about it.

The claim was made by Laura A. Fleming, owner of land near Oklahoma City that was involved in an oil and gas lease dispute. She said O. A. Cargill, Sr., had told her in his law office, "I've got a majority of that (supreme) court fixed just like I had Van Meter fixed...from Chief Justice Corn on down." (Van Meter was in reference to District Judge A. P. Van Meter.)

The issue arose out of a dispute over sale of a mineral lease on the Fleming farm. Mrs. Fleming and her husband were called to Cargill's office, where he sought to buy their mineral lease for $1,200 plus $500 for their expenses. When they refused, stating that they had already been offered $8,000, Cargill became angry and blurted out that they couldn't possibly win in court because he controlled the court.

The complete text of Mrs. Fleming's affidavit printed in the plaintiff's brief and filed with the state supreme court April 7, 1948, was printed in the *Oklahoma City Times*. It was indicative of the way Cargill worked:

"I, Mrs. Laura A. Fleming, state that on the 28th day of April, 1944, a district court case was heard before Judge A. P. Van Meter in Oklahoma County; *Laura A. Fleming v. D. L. Kelly*, involving a purported contract for the purchase of an oil and gas lease on our farm in the West Edmond oil field. My attorney in that case was Mr. Fred L. Hoyt; Mr. Kelly was represented by Mr. Sam Montgomery, who said he was trying the case for Mr. O. A. Cargill. We lost that case and the record speaks for itself.

"On or about the second day of May, 1944, only four or five days after this case was tried, Mr. D. L. Kelly came out to where we lived on West 10th St. and told us Mr. O. A. Cargill wanted us both to come to his office in the Hales Building to see him.

"We suggested getting our attorney, Mr. Fred L. Hoyt, to go with us. Mr. Kelly said: 'No,' that Mr. Cargill just wanted to see us privately and confidentially without our attorney. We then suggested we telephone Mr. Hoyt and tell him Mr. Cargill wanted us to come to his office, but Mr. Kelly insisted that Mr. Cargill wanted to see us alone and hear his proposition before we told anything to our lawyer. We therefore, and at Mr. Kelly's insistence, went to see Mr. O. A. Cargill in his office.

"In Mr. O. A. Cargill's office were Mr. Cargill, Mr. Kelly, my husband and myself.

"Mr. Cargill started the conversation by saying:

'Now folks, the reason I sent Mr. Kelly to bring you here without your lawyer was not because I dislike Fred Hoyt, for really Fred is a fine little fellow, but I wanted to try to work out a trade with you on that lease on your farm.

'I have several farms out there and I know all of those other farmers and they all know me...I get things done for them and they know it.

'Of course, you realize that you lost your case in district court...We knew you'd lose it before the case was tried...I mean that confidentially and with no disrespect to your lawyer.'

"Mr. Cargill offered us $1,200 for our lease if we would not let our lawyer appeal the case to the supreme court, plus $500 to help pay our expenses while we were down here from our home in Detroit, Michigan.

"We refused this offer and told him he knew that we had sold the lease for $8,000 cash and could get our money as soon as we could get Kelly's false affidavit off the record, for it clouded our title.

"Mr. Cargill then said:

'Well, if you want to be foolish enough to let some lawyer talk you into appealing this case, I can keep you in supreme court for four or five years and of course I know you wouldn't want that, for by that time there'd be wells drilled all around your land and all the oil will be drained from under it; then even I wouldn't want your lease--not at the price I'm offering you today, and chances are I wouldn't want it for $12 much less $1,200.'

"Mr. Cargill seemed to go into a rage of temper saying:

'I guess you folks really don't know who I am. To begin with, I represent Kelly in this lawsuit, but in reality that lease is mine, and that was my money that Kelly gave you, and I've got more money besides that $100 tied up in this thing, and I certainly don't intend to lose it. Maybe you folks had better look around and see just how many important lawsuits O. A. Cargill loses in these courts around here.'

"Mr. Fleming then said:

'Mr. Cargill, if that's your lease and your lawsuit and you are that much interested in getting that lease, then why didn't you come in court down there yourself?'

"Mr. Cargill got mad again, stood up and waving his arms said:

'I didn't have to be in court for the trial. Looks like I did a pretty good job representing Mr. Kelly in this case. Why I tried that case several days before in Judge Van Meter's private office...'

"And Mr. Cargill shouted: 'Let me tell you something else...you saw how you lost your case in district court, well, you'll lose a damn sight worse in the supreme court because I've got a majority of that court fixed just like I had Van Meter fixed...from Chief Justice Corn on down, and there are nine judges out there. Now you folks better think that over while I'm in the notion to give you $1,200 plus $500 expenses."[18]

When contacted by a reporter, Cargill said he had never heard of the affidavit "until this very minute." He termed the statements in it "the wildest, most unreasonable thing I have ever heard in my life."[19] Cargill admitted he had drilled two oil wells on the property, but he professed not to remember how he got title to it.

Reached in his office, Judge Van Meter said he had no recollection of the Fleming case and there was nothing about it that he could recall without checking the records. He declared categorically: "There wasn't any deal made in chambers about anything."[20]

Nevertheless, Fleming's affidavit made an important point. It showed that apart from whether or not Cargill had the court "fixed," as he claimed, the very fact that he was able to say that--and cause people to believe it--told a lot about the public's confidence in the integrity of the court, or lack thereof. Moreover, Cargill's outburst showed that whenever the public believes the courts *can* be fixed, that becomes a tool in the hands of an unscrupulous lawyer who wants to manipulate someone into an unwise decision, or create the image of a man who "gets things done."

Harry L. S. Halley, chief justice of the supreme court, appeared before the house investigating committee on Wednesday, March 3. He told the committee that Corn "did his best" to campaign for a decision favoring Selected Investments Corp. "Corn seemed quite interested in the case...because of his friends in Dewey County," Halley testified.[21]

Halley, himself, did not vote on the case. He said that he was friendly with Phil Burns, one of Selected's officers and another man involved in the case. "I just didn't vote," Halley said.[22]

In more than an hour's testimony, Halley denied personal knowledge of any bribes paid to any member of the high court. "There is nothing in my experience to show that a member of our court has taken a bribe," he said.

Committee chairman Allard tried to get Halley to say that Justice Welch had not been carrying a normal work load in recent months. Allard and some committee members had been looking into the possibility of impeaching Welch on grounds of neglect of duty. However, those hopes received a setback when Halley testified that Welch's office had written 17 opinions since April of the previous year, which was pretty close to his normal case load.

Allard took the occasion to lecture the court for not taking steps to clear itself of rumors that have been floating around the state for years. "The court ought to do something about things like that," he said.[23]

Justices Johnson and Welch were next on the committee's docket. For them, something *was* about to be done.

5

Moving to Impeach

In his first public appearance since having been under fire, Justice N. B. Johnson went before the house committee at 10:00 a.m. on Tuesday, March 9. Burke Mordy, chief counsel for the house investigations committee, led the questioning.

Testifying under oath, Johnson flatly denied to the committee that he had ever accepted a bribe or had knowledge of a bribe being paid to a member of the supreme court. The 17-year veteran on the court also denied he had ever drank intoxicants during working hours or that any undue pressure had been applied to him in regard to any case.

In answer to questions concerning former Justice Corn, Johnson asked to examine an 84-page statement Corn gave to federal authorities. ''Do you have the statement?'' Johnson asked Mordy.

''I'm not at liberty to discuss that,'' Mordy said.

At one point, Johnson attacked Corn as a ''self-confessed criminal...vilifying members of the court.'' He said he knew of three witnesses who would testify that Corn told them he never paid money to any member of the high court. When Mordy pressed him for the names of the witnesses, Johnson named himself, Judge Welch and Tulsa attorney Floyd Rheem.[1]

Reference was made to an apparent accusation that Johnson had used intoxicants during working hours. ''If any statement were made that you were seen in an intoxicated condition during working hours, what would your answer be?'' he was asked.

"That would be incorrect," Johnson said.[2]

Johnson was asked if he would submit to a polygraph examination in regard to whether he had used intoxicants during working hours, as well as other charges. He said he would consult his attorney. "I never believed in those very much. I reserve my answer on that," Johnson replied.[3]

Burke Mordy urged Johnson to assent, saying, "...it would greatly help this committee if you would submit to a polygraph examination." He asked Johnson to give his answer by 5:00 p.m. the following day.

In other testimony, Johnson was queried at length about apparent testimony given to the Oklahoma bar committee by R. O. Ingle, Johnson's legal assistant for 12 years, former state senator, and now an attorney with the Oklahoma Tax Commission. The questions centered on a series of legal cases that had been before the court.

Johnson was also asked about campaign contributions. He acknowledged that he did receive campaign contributions in 1954 and 1960 even though he had no opponents and made no campaign expenditures. "Would you say you received $100 or $1,000 in those two years," asked a committee member.[4]

"I would say I received that much," Johnson answered.

Referring to O. A. Cargill, Sr., Johnson said he never received campaign contributions from the attorney. When asked if he was a personal friend of Cargill, Johnson replied, "Not a close friend--I knew him." He also acknowledged that he had been in Cargill's home.[5]

In the judgment of veteran reporter Jim Young of the *Daily Oklahoman*, "Johnson was the most vague witness the house committee had heard since it started interviewing the judges. It was often necessary for questions to be repeated. Many questions brought an 'I don't remember'."[6]

Whatever qualities Johnson lost in vagueness, Welch more than made up in feistiness. Taking the stand in his own defense on Wednesday, the diminutive justice repeatedly engaged in verbal sparring bouts with his questioners.

Welch called on the committee to release an 84-page statement made by Corn. "I believe the people are entitled to see that statement," Welch declared. He said there could be only four reasons for withholding the statement: "It is being concealed either to help someone, or to hurt someone, or to keep from hurting someone, or to keep from helping someone." [7]

Welch said he believed the statement in its entirety would give some clue as to Corn's motives in accusing Welch and Johnson with bribery. "He (Corn) must have wanted out of that place more than anything on earth," Welch suggested.

One representative asked Welch if he could think of any reason Corn would make a statement about paying Welch a bribe. "I think you're coming now to speculate on what was in Judge Corn's mind when he made that statement," Welch said. "It is too horribly speculative."[8]

Questioned by other committeemen, Judge Welch said it was not true that Corn had told him that he and Johnson should resign from the court. He testified that he received a "confused" letter from Corn while the latter was in the federal prison hospital in Springfield. He said the letter informed him: "I have disclosed to the county attorney and to the federal attorney the facts in the *Selected Investments* case and the *Westbrook* case. I am under an order not to talk to you."[9]

Welch said he identified the *Selected Investments* case, but he found no record of a "Westbrook" case. Committee counsel asked, "Isn't Westcott the name of the son-in-law of Cargill? Did you ever try to determine if he meant Westcott instead of Westbrook?"

"That simply shows how confused Corn was," snapped Welch.

Welch flatly denied he had ever received a bribe. He also denied knowing of any bribes paid to other justices or being aware of any undue influence directed at members of the court.

In other testimony, Welch acknowledged receiving several campaign contributions from O. A. Cargill. He said that Cargill contributed to his campaign "at least two or three times," and he estimated the contributions at between $200 and $400. When asked if Cargill ever asked for anything in return, Welch replied: "Absolutely not!"

The committee also asked if Welch had received contributions from Ned Looney. Welch said Looney had contributed to his campaigns.

Fireworks flew with regard to Corn's 84-page statement. Welch asserted, "An untrue story like that can't live and stand the light of day."

Mordy challenged Welch to take a lie detector test, but Welch refused to agree, all the while insisting he was not saying "no." The justice insisted that polygraph examinations are "uncertain" and "would not settle anything."

"Let the record reflect it is my understanding the judge said 'No,'" Mordy said.

"Let the record show that if he (Mordy) does not understand my answer it should be read to him," Welch retorted.[10]

On two occasions, Welch hinted he might make a deal with the committee to take a polygraph test. "I might make you a proposition," Welch told Mordy. "If we could also pick out a couple of witnesses and let me pick them, then after seeing the results and observing the thing work, I might agree."

When Mordy asked Welch to name the witnesses, the justice added another stipulation: "...And if you would agree that no bribery charges would be brought against me or no action by this legislature...."[11]

Welch criticized the committee for requesting he take a lie detector test. He asked Mordy to withdraw the request. "I will not withdraw the request," Mordy said.[12]

In a strongly worded statement, committee chairman Allard informed Welch, "During the present investigation, this committee intends to make no deals or act on any 'proposition'."[13]

Thursday, March 11, the house committee received word that Justice N. B. Johnson refused to submit to a polygraph examination as requested, citing legal objections and his health as reasons.

"I would not be reluctant to consent to a polygraphic test if it would serve any useful probative value," Johnson said. "But such tests do not prove or disprove anything and are not acceptable in the courts, absent any stipulation or agreement to use it."[14]

The investigation committee also heard testimony from Justice Ben T. Williams that he once received, indirectly, a $25,000 offer in connection with a case before the supreme court. Williams said the offer was made through his father, John F. Williams, who died in 1955. The case involved a $1.5 million estate. Williams said he reported the offer to other members of the court, but nothing came of it.

The 12-year veteran of the court declined to name in open session the persons his father said approached him with the $25,000 offer. Members took him behind closed doors, and after a short closed session Rep. Allard reported that Williams had supplied two names.

Justice Williams said he had no personal knowledge of any bribe being paid to any member of the court or of any bribe being offered a member of the court.

Tuesday, March 16 testimony was highlighted with a trip to the home of R. O. Ingle, Justice Johnson's former legal assistant. The committee questioned Ingle from his living room divan shortly before he was to enter the hospital for treatment of a respiratory ailment.

Ingle told the committee that Johnson was easily under the influence of Justice Earl Welch. He also said that the late Justice Lon Carlile was under Welch's influence while he was on the court.

Ingle related an incident that occurred following court disposition of a case known as *Eastern Torpedo v. Price*. Ingle said he met the late attorney Tom Waldrop at the state capitol and Waldrop offered him a ride to town. He said that Waldrop told him, "We owe you a thousand dollars. We know the hard work you did in this case *(Eastern Torpedo)*."

Ingle said he declined the offer saying, "You don't owe me anything."

He said Waldrop answered, "I gave Welch $10,000 and if you say anything about it, it's a ____ lie."[15]

Ingle told the committee that in 1956 two men came to Justice Johnson's office and conferred with the judge. Ingle said later he "became reasonably certain" that one of the men was W. H. "Pat" O'Bryan, then an attorney for Selected Investments, and he was not sure if the other man was Hugh Carroll, president of Selected.

The former legal aide said that as the men left the "judge came out and pitched a brief on my desk and suggested the case should be reversed."

Ingle said the brief was filed that day by Selected setting out its arguments in the lawsuit with the state tax commission. The former aide said the statement was made at a time when the tax commission had 40 days to file its answering brief.

Ingle continued, "It was my opinion that on this morning he (Johnson) had been drinking." He said on two or three other occasions he felt that the judge had been drinking, but added, "This was after 5 o'clock."[16]

Ingle also was quoted as saying that Justice Welch tended to favor cases that were being handled by attorney members of his family. He said that although Welch disqualified himself from participating in court action, he "campaigned" on their behalf among other justices.

On their way back to the capitol after interviewing Ingle, the committee called on former Justice Corn at his home. Corn inspected a signed 84-page statement in which he admitted accepting a bribe and implicated two other justices in sharing in a $150,000 payoff. Corn verified the lengthy statement as being the one he made shortly before leaving the federal prison in December and also verified his notarized signature.

Rep. Allard said Corn, now 81, convinced the committee he was in top mental condition, although reported ailing physically.

"I've never seen a man 80-plus who had his wits about him any better," the committee chairman said.[17]

Earlier Tuesday, the committee heard from LaNoah Angelly, who was the plaintiff in a damage suit against Magnolia Petroleum Company. Angelly was burned in 1947 by an explosion of an airplane he was gassing at the Antlers airport. His attorney was Lee Welch, brother of Justice Welch. Angelly estimated he received approximately $20,000 from the award of $88,468, and was rooked out of the rest by Lee Welch.

Angelly, dressed in tattered clothes and accompanied by his wife and two young children, testified that at one time he asked Lee Welch about the money, but the Antlers attorney told him, "We had some friends to take care of." Angelly said he asked who the friends were "and he dismissed the subject."[18]

A chart showing "an interesting pattern" in voting similarities among the justices was introduced by committee chairman Allard. The chart dealt with eight cases repeatedly mentioned during previous questioning of high court justices.

Allard said the vote pattern showed the following:

* In six of the eight cases, Welch, Corn and Johnson voted exactly the same.

* In two cases, Welch did not vote because they involved his lawyer-relatives; but in both, his appointed replacement voted the same way Johnson and Corn did.

* In seven of the eight cases, two or three of the trio were in the winning majority. In the eighth case, the Meadors will, the trio voted together as a three-judge block, dissenting minority.

* In only one case did Corn's vote differ from Johnson's and Welch's; and in that instance, Corn's vote did not change the outcome.

It was also interesting to hear some of the dissenting opinions in these cases.

In the *Oklahoma Company v. O'Neil* suit, of which Harold Westcott, son-in-law of attorney O. A. Cargill, Sr., was president of Oklahoma Co., a $35,364 judgment was reversed in favor of Oklahoma Co. The vote was 5 to 4 with Justices Williams, Halley, Blackbird and Jackson dissenting. In a withering dissenting opinion, Justice Halley called Westcott "the mastermind" of a plan to "defraud" his partners. He referred to Westcott as "an experienced oil man of the promoter type," and added: "Working under the guise of a friend, he fast-talked the defendants into purchasing an interest....The evidence is clear that no sooner than Westcott began operating the properties, he began to defraud his partners.

"The majority opinion justifies the unconscionable conduct of Westcott...the great weight of the evidence sustains the trial court decision. The entire transaction is so shot-through with fraud and deception that I am of the opinion that the judgment of the trial court is the only way this case can be properly disposed of."[19]

In the *Selected Investments Corp.* case, Justice Welch wrote the opinion which reversed the case in favor of Selected, thereby saving the firm nearly $200,000 in state income taxes plus an undisclosed amount of federal taxes. Cargill was the attorney for the firm. Corn and Johnson voted with the majority. The dissenting opinion was written by Justice Jackson and concurred in by Justice Blackbird. Justice Halley did not vote because he had friends involved in the case.

Welch disqualified himself from the *Magnolia Petroleum Co. v. Angelly* case, in which his brother, Lee Welch, represented Angelly. The high court upheld the judgment in a 5 to 4 vote with Corn and Johnson voting in favor, along with Welch's appointed replacement. Justice Williams wrote a dissenting opinion, in which Justices Halley, Blackbird and Jackson concurred. Justice Williams wrote that there was no evidence offered by the plaintiff (Angelly) to show that gasoline or vapor leaked from Magnolia equipment. He said the plaintiff "wholly failed to establish primary negligence" on which the case was based against the oil company.[20]

Another case talked about was *Marshall v. Amos* involving a dispute over oil and gas royalties reversed by the supreme court, knocking down a judgment H. D. Amos and Sinclair Oil & Gas Co. won against Ida B. and H. G. Marshall. Voting to reverse were Justices Welch, Johnson and Corn, along with Justices Halley and Blackbird.

Rep. Allard also discussed *Johnson v. Johnson*, a disputed will case in which both county and district courts denied admission to probate of a will left by Dexter B. Johnson. Voting to reverse the lower courts were Justices Johnson, Welch, Corn, Arnold and Blackbird. Justice Halley wrote a dissenting opinion. Halley wrote that the disputed document was not executed according to law, was a typed, and not a handwritten document, and was not signed, dated or witnessed. ''A casual inspection reveals this is not itself a will,'' he wrote. ''Without the handwriting of the testator, it is only a scrap of paper.''[21]

There was also the personal injury case of *Jordan Bus Co. v. Wafer*, represented by relatives of Justice Welch--Hal Welch, Don Welch and Don E. Welch, who won a $75,000 default judgment against Jordan. Justice Welch disqualified himself. Voting in favor of the Wafers were Justices Johnson, Corn, Arnold, O'Neal, and Welch's replacement, the late Robert Perdue of Wilburton, Oklahoma. Again, Justice Halley wrote the dissent, saying that a gross injustice was done the company. He also noted that briefs filed in the case disclosed that an offer had been made by the Wafers to drop the suit for $5,000.

Embattled attorney O. A. Cargill refused to answer questions when called before the investigating committee on Thursday, March 18. Cargill, flanked by a son, two grandsons and an attorney, appeared under subpoena. He produced a telegram from his attorney Percy Foreman, Houston, Texas, who was then on a case in Chicago.

The attorney wired, ''You are advised to claim your constitutional right to remain silent when you respond to the subpoena of this state legislative committee....'' Foreman said to testify while Cargill's federal case was pending would be grossly improper.[22]

The committee then went into an executive session with Cargill.

Earlier Thursday, the committee listened for a little more than an hour to Lee Welch, Antlers attorney and brother of Justice Earl Welch, as he sought to explain where the money went in the Angelly case. He insisted that Angelly got "something in excess of 50 percent" of the division of the money after expenses were taken out. He recounted that $4,500 went to one nephew, $5,000 to another nephew, and $15,000 to disbarred attorney Tom Waldrop.

"Wasn't that an exorbitant fee?" Burke G. Mordy, committee counsel, asked.

"That's a matter of opinion," Lee Welch said. The Antlers attorney was unable to produce any canceled checks or other financial records.[23]

After hearing its last witness, Thursday, March 18, 1965, the house investigation committee went into executive session where it approved articles recommending the impeachment of Justices Earl Welch and N. B. Johnson. The full house was scheduled to receive the Articles of Impeachment on Monday, and it was expected to set Wednesday for the vote.

Three articles were voted against Welch and two against Johnson. Welch was charged with taking a $7,500 bribe in the *Selected Investments* tax case, for taking a $2,500 bribe in a 1957 case involving a dispute over a Washington County oil lease involving O. A. Cargill's son-in-law, Harold Westcott, and for his conviction in federal court on income tax evasion.

Johnson was charged for taking a $7,500 bribe in the *Selected Investments* case and a $2,500 bribe in the Washington County lease case.

Just hours before the house investigating committee filed Articles of Impeachment against him and Justice Johnson, Justice Welch submitted his resignation, thus bringing a sad end to a career on the high court that began back in 1932. Welch was the senior justice on the court.

Welch stepped down from the court with a long letter to

Governor Bellmon proclaiming his innocence, decrying ''hear-say'' evidence, and blasting the press. Welch wrote in his resignation letter:

''Historically, under our system of government, the power of the government has been divided into the three separate departments:

1. Legislative
2. Executive, and
3. Judicial.

''Fundamentally, this is as it should be, and I would not entertain any proposal to alter these fundamental principles of the government of a free people.

''Under this system, the power to investigate, to accuse and impeach any state public official lies within the hands of, and under the control of the legislative department, whereby the House of Representatives may investigate and accuse, and the Senate shall act as the tribunal before whom any impeachment charge is to be tried. This is the law of our nation, which we all love.

''Now, whether it be right or wrong, the practice has grown up, and, so far as I know has been generally accepted, in all states of this nation, of permitting witnesses to testify to things they say they have heard from others, whether the ''others'' are dead or alive, which is nothing more than what is known as ''hearsay evidence.''

''Witnesses may testify as to what they think, and all of this without any investigation or determination of the character or reliability of the person whom the witness purports to quote.

''Of course, this type of testimony is repugnant to the legal mind, and is never admissible in a court of law in either a civil or a criminal prosecution.

''Affidavits are never admissible in evidence of fact in the trial of any case, civil or criminal, in any of the courts of the land.

All of this type of testimony before an investigating committee, and in an impeachment trial, may be fitting and proper, because, as has been said, these proceedings are 'political' and not 'judicial.'

"However, the enormity of the harm, which can and does result from these rules of evidence, is not to be laid at the door of the Legislature, but actually comes about because the proceedings are public and the newspaper reporters, looking for sensational news, and the newspapers for whom they work, whose interest, at least in part, is in selling more papers, feel the fact that this type of evidence is a part of public records, they are at liberty to publish and distribute, throughout the state and elsewhere, with complete immunity, such hearsay evidence, which may or may not have been given to the witness by wholly irresponsible and reckless people.

"Even a member of the Legislature, in either the House of Representatives or in the Senate, may make from the floor, while in session, the most defamatory statements with complete immunity for reckless indiscretion and character assassination.

"As a lawyer, a judge who has been elected for a total of 44 years, and a continuing student of the law, all of these factors present a problem to me which I actually cannot comprehend.

"It is so foreign to the manner of presentation, arguments and determination of issues, of fact, and law, in courts of justice, that all of it is incomprehensible to me, and I think to any conscientious student of the law.

Frankly, I do not feel that after a lifetime in the legal profession, I am able to cope with this type of proceedings.

"I have been accused by affidavits, hearsay evidence and innuendo, but not by a witness. This type of evidence has been circulated throughout my state by some, but not all, of the leading newspapers.

"I have concluded that it is as impossible for me to cope with this type of proceedings as it was for the small child who was caught repeating gossip and was told by her mother that the only way she could rectify her wrong would be to split open a pillow and allow the feathers to escape to the four winds and then retrieve every single feather.

"Not unmindful, but deeply appreciative of the loyalty of my many friends among laymen, bench, and the bar, and with the hope that I will have their continued respect and friendship, I have concluded to, and I do hereby resign from the office of Justice of the Supreme Court of Oklahoma, effective immediately.

"In conclusion, I want to say that I do not admit, but emphatically deny, guilt of any of the many rumors, published affidavits, and hearsay evidence, which have been circulated under the guise of news and reports of public hearings.

"The 'power of the press' under the guise of 'freedom of speech' has attained another victory, and I humbly bow to what appears to me to be the inevitable, in submitting this resignation, with the hope that I, now 73 years of age, may live the remainder of my life in peace and dignity."[24]

Justice N. B. Johnson protested his innocence and said he would not resign because he was not guilty.

The upcoming house vote the following Wednesday was by no means a foregone conclusion. Rep. William Briscoe of Claremore argued forcefully that there was no witness to support Corn's allegation that he paid Johnson $7,500 in one case, $2,500 in another. Briscoe charged that Corn was in prison at the time and "his chief interest was to get out of prison."[25]

Much was said in the debate concerning the lack of corroborating evidence. Those who spoke against voting the impeachment made much of the lack of a witness to the actual money changing hands. Rep. Phil Smalley, member of the investigating committee, responded to the critics, saying: "You're never going to find anybody bribing these judges in the presence of witnesses."[26]

Several members demanded that the committee present its evidence before they considered impeachment. Committee chairman Allard insisted that the house action was not a criminal proceeding, and a presentation of the evidence prior to an ouster trial in the senate would tip their hand. "Either the house believes in the committee system or it doesn't," Allard said. "If they don't, then they can forget it."[27]

Justice Corn emerged as the likely key to the debate. "We can get the money to Corn," Allard said, "but Corn is the only eyeball witness who links the money to Johnson."[28]

When the vote was taken, the Oklahoma House of Representatives approved the Articles of Impeachment of Justice Johnson. In votes of 90-6 and 88-8, the house approved the two charges against the high court justice and sent them on to the senate.

The senate was already preparing for action. Within minutes of receiving the articles, the upper chamber voted to suspend Justice Johnson pending the outcome of the impeachment trial.

As if the embattled justice didn't already have trouble enough, his woes multiplied two days later. Saturday, March 27, the Oklahoma County grand jury returned indictments on him on bribery charges.

6

Anatomy of an Election

(As it was then)

The shocking revelations of wrongdoing on the high court caused people to ask how it was possible for justice to be bought and sold on a "cash and carry" basis. How could these men who were charged with the highest responsibility for interpreting the law allow themselves to get caught up in the very acts of greed and corruption they were sworn to proscribe?

Oklahoma's election process allowed plenty of opportunity for cutting deals and coming under the influence of power brokers.

"A scandal just waiting to happen," is how many critics characterized the state's method of selecting supreme court justices in that era. The process was old-fashioned partisan politics, pure and simple. Each political party mounted its candidates for the supreme court in much the same manner as they elected legislators and other political officers.

Procedurally, about the only difference was the practice of nominating supreme court candidates from "nominating districts." It was a "hybrid" election process. The candidate first had to get the party nomination in his home nominating district, including any run-off primaries. However, unlike a state legislator who was elected by the people within his home district, a supreme court nominee then ran at-large in the state-wide general elections.

An appraisal of Oklahoma's judicial districts in 1958, the year of my election, would indicate a strong imbalance in favor of the rural counties. Of the total nine judicial districts, two were urban (Tulsa and Oklahoma City) and seven were rural.

Clearly, the districts which had the larger lawyer populations gave voters a wider selection. Interestingly, the two urban districts of Tulsa and Oklahoma City with 1,300 and 1,700 lawyers, respectively, *each* had as many practicing lawyers from which to nominate as did all *seven rural districts combined.*[1] Contrast this with District 4, the Panhandle, in which the choice was limited to just 121 lawyers. Presumably, a wider choice would result in better candidates from which to choose.

My personal odyssey to the high court can serve as an illustration of how the process worked at that time. Although I cannot claim that it reflects the situation of all judges, it nevertheless can serve as a platform, or "case study," to highlight some of the problems and pitfalls that were built into the system.

In the first place, the qualities desired in a candidate for elective office are not necessarily the qualities most desired in an impartial judge. Many of the most studious and capable judges find it very difficult to "sell" themselves the way a political candidate has to. Some find the idea to be very demeaning. Further, the necessity to finance and run a campaign, to take stands and define issues, often tempts the prospective judge to make compromises and may expose him to corrosive influences.

Tulsa attorney Jack Hays outlined the capriciousness of the state's political method for electing judges in an article for the *Tulsa Law Journal.* He recalled the story that Justice Harry L. S. Halley had been defeated in 1946 in a bid for re-election as a district judge in Tulsa. Just two years later, Halley managed to get himself elected to the state's supreme court.

"No one can possibly justify this (seeming contradiction) on the basis of voter intelligence," Hays remarked. "Justice Halley jokingly says in 1946 he was such a poor judge the voters retired him, and in 1948 he was such a good judge the voters put him on the supreme court."[2]

My situation bore some interesting parallels to Hays's

characterization of Halley's election. In 1953, I was first appointed to the bench as county judge in Oklahoma County. I asked for, and was assigned to, the juvenile division.

In my capacity as county judge in charge of juveniles, I built quite a reputation for improving the juvenile court system. For example, during the five-year period I made more than 300 speeches to various civic and community groups, ranging from church groups to parent-teacher associations, to any group that would ask for a county judge to speak. My goal was to get the community involved to help with juvenile delinquents. I never considered myself a good speaker, but I was convincing and sincere, and my message was accepted.

I pushed very strongly the idea of a juvenile detention home and I worked hard to get enabling legislation passed to construct one. These community efforts paid off. The center was eventually built and named "The Berry House" in my honor.

All was not peaches and cream, however. During the 1956 political season I got caught between the proverbia "rock and a hard place." Two friends, Granville Scanland and James W. "Bill" Berry were both vying for the same office as Oklahoma County Attorney. Both sides were actively seeking my support, but I wanted no part of it. Lined up on Scanland's side was George Miskovsky, flamboyant attorney, state senator and aspiring candidate for governor; and on the other was my wife's cousin. Professionally, I felt it would be improper in my position as a judge to come out publicly in support of either candidate, so I decided to remain neutral. Unfortunately, as one might expect, I ended up alienating both sides. Miskovsky, through an intermediary, threatened me with reprisal if I didn't get behind Scanland. I said to him, "I'm going on a vacation. I'm doing nothing." When the ballots were counted, James W. Berry was elected, and Miskovsky's candidate lost.

The next thing I knew, Miskovsky was working to get a bill through the legislature to create a new juvenile judge position that would have greatly expanded authority, including control over all the juvenile officers. This would be a nice political position and I naturally assumed that with the recognition and esteem I had gained throughout the county as an advocate of juvenile justice, I would be the logical recipient of that position. That was in 1958.

But it was not to be. Through the lobbying efforts of a powerful legislator, another person was appointed to the position that I thought should have been mine. That is not to disparage the new judge, Homer Smith, who turned out to be a very fine judge; nevertheless, my being passed over for an appointment which I felt I had earned was a bitter disappointment.

For a while, I considered going back into private practice. Then I got to thinking, *My goodness, why don't I run for another office?* Earlier, in 1950, I had made an unsuccessful run for congress, being narrowly defeated by John Jarman. That campaign, plus my five years in the public eye as a county judge, had given me a taste for the political trail.

The big question was, *which* office? My thoughts led me to consider the supreme court. Judge W. A. ("Lon") Carlile, a mid-term appointee from District 3, Oklahoma City, was up for re-election that year. Asking the opinion of a number of attorneys who practiced before the supreme court I determined that Carlile was vulnerable. He was perceived as a nice old man, genuine and outgoing, well-liked by everybody, but really not much of a factor on the high court.

The "book" on Carlile was that his appointment was repayment for a political debt owed by Ned Looney, one of the two or three most powerful attorneys in Oklahoma City. Subsequently, when a vacancy occurred on the supreme court upon the death of Justice Albert Hunt, Ned Looney went to work to help get Carlile placed on the court by Governor Raymond Gary. Carlile, at the time of his appointment, was well up into his sixties and generally thought to be a little old for an initial appointment. In appearance, he seemed even older than his years because his health was quite frail and he walked with a feeble shuffle.

In his capacity as a justice, Carlile had a reputation of always trying to be very fair. His major weakness, however, was that he was perceived to be overly anxious to be loyal to his old friends. In my opinion, such loyalty might be considered an asset in political office, but on the court it was a liability, in that it might tend to color the judge's legal opinion.

Despite Carlile's vulnerability, the answers I consistently got back about my own chances for election were not encouraging. People said, "You can't do it because Ned Looney and O. A. Cargill run politics. They name the judges."

Nevertheless, there was an obstinate streak in me, and the more times I heard that refrain the more it got my dander up. I decided that was a situation that could be broken and I decided to give it my best effort.

Shortly after announcing my candidacy, I happened to run into Ned Looney in the lobby of First National Bank. Somewhat tongue-in-cheek, I asked him, "By the way, Mr. Looney, I'm going to run for the supreme court. Will you support me?"

"I'll tell you what," Looney replied, "you run, and I'm going to do everything in my power to beat you."

I just laughed. "I'm going to do it, and I'll do it without spending any more money than you do. You just tell me how much you want to spend and I won't go over that amount."

"No, I will not!" Looney retorted. "But we are going to beat you!" He emphasized the word *we*.

The *Daily Oklahoman* referred to the race between Carlile and me as a "popularity contest." At age 42, I was much younger and more vigorous. Carlile, on the other hand, was getting old and feeble, and it was difficult for him to walk across a room without help. Accordingly, Carlile's strategy was to avoid as much as possible any joint appearances where the two of us would appear on the platform together.

There were eight counties that made up the third judicial district: Alfalfa, Blaine, Canadian, Garfield, Grant, Kingfisher, Logan, and Oklahoma. The area had a population of 575,000.

Both of us ran on the Democratic ticket. This meant that--given the weakness of the Republican party--the race would be won or lost in the primary.

The traditional form of campaigning was for the candidate to make the rounds of the various towns and cities in the district and to contact the most influential person in that area. Then, having secured that person's commitment, to rely on that person's influence to carry the county.

Obviously, that approach of basing one's campaign so largely on gaining the support of power brokers can open oneself to certain risks. Among other things, the candidate was at the mercy of the power broker for whatever promises, or "deal cutting," the power broker might exact in exchange for his commitment to deliver the votes in his area.

To cite an example, I was approached by a prominent Oklahoma City banker at a dinner party. With several people standing nearby, the banker propositioned me point blank, "Bill, if you are elected on that court, would you let me come and visit you, go in and close the door and talk about my lawsuit--not to influence you, but I think certain things should be told to you which may not be allowed into evidence and may not be a part of the record. Would you give me that privilege, and then you just vote your conscience?"

I told him, "I won't. I can't do it. If I did that, I would have to let the other side come in, and I don't know where we would end up."

"Why won't you?" the banker asked.

"Because there is over 300 years of judicial ethics that tell me I shouldn't do that."

Taken aback, the banker replied. "Well, there are a lot better judges in this county and state than you are, and they would let me do it."

I responded with a touch of sarcasm, "Well, when I get to be that good a judge, perhaps then I'll let you do that. But I won't do it until then."

"I am still going to vote for you," the banker stated as he

turned to leave, "but I am not going to support you other than that. I am not going to tell anybody one way or the other how to vote, but I will help you only with my personal vote."

Nevertheless, I felt that I had earned a few converts from the people standing nearby because of holding my position against this prominent banker. At least, that is what some of them reported to me later.

Running for office exposes a judge to all kinds of temptations, particularly when it comes to financing the campaign. Sometimes it could be hard for even the most honest of judges to separate a genuine campaign contribution from a covert attempt to influence the court.

One illuminating example occurred at the time Justice Corn was sentenced to prison. U.S. District Attorney B. Andrew Potter said he had a witness who would testify that the bribe was to go to Corn and "others" for "campaign expenses." Obviously, it would be a convenient dodge for a temptation-prone judge to receive money in the guise of "campaign contributions." Under this category, any extra illicit income would be almost impossible to trace.

Justice Ben T. Williams, who was never implicated in any scandal, told house probers of a bribe offer that he once received. Indirectly, a $25,000 offer in connection with a case before the supreme court was made through his father, John F. Williams.[2]

According to Williams, the offer was for a $25,000 campaign contribution in connection with the *Meadors* will case which involved a $1.3 million estate. Williams turned down the $25,000 offer. "It would just not be right," he told his father.

He reported that his father, a rural mail carrier, said to him, "Golly, that sounds like all the money in the world."

Williams reported the $25,000 offer to other members of the court at the time it was reported to him. However, he said that he declined to tell the justices who had made the offer to his father.

Probably a more common approach is one related by Justice Floyd L. Jackson in which he may have received an improper approach from an attorney. According to Jackson, the attorney offered to aid him in a campaign and then suggested the judge might need the money to help him in trips back to his home district.

"It is the only time since I have been a judge that I ever had a chance to receive money," Jackson said.[3]

I made up my mind that rather than deal with the power brokers, I would run a people-to-people campaign. For me it was more beneficial to shake hands with fifty people than it was to make a speech to fifty people. By shaking hands, giving them literature and asking for their support, that one little contact would stay with them all the way to the polling booth. Accordingly, I went around to as many doors as I could, visited as many factories and businesses as I could, and shook as many hands as I could. Of course, I did make my share of speeches, but I didn't rely on the speeches to deliver the votes.

Other kinds of "deals" were offered to me as well. My brother-in-law, Jim Arrington, a long-time member of the legislature from Payne County, came to me with an interesting proposition. Arrington said that he had been approached by an influential lawyer who said that if we could come up with $10,000, he could get Carlile to withdraw from the campaign. My immediate response was to say, "That's against the law!"

Arrington hurried to explain that he was just an emissary who was conveying the message because he was asked to, not because he wanted to. "The way it was presented to me," he said, "is that the state has no retirement program for members of the supreme court. Recently, in the legislature we enacted a bill that would partially remedy that situation. Under this new rule, when a justice retires voluntarily, he would be allowed to remain on the court as a 'supernumerary' judge to help out with the court's business and get rid of the case load; and thus they would draw a pittance of pay which doesn't amount to much. But even that provision applies only if the judge *voluntarily* leaves the office.

So Carlile's friends gave him bad advice when they persuaded him to abandon the privilege of becoming a supernumerary justice in order to run for re-election. If it turns out that Carlile loses, he's out on the street...out of a job...and not eligible for supernumerary pay."

"Well, Jim," I declared flatly, "it's against the law, and that's all there is to it!"

"Well, I brought you the information. I didn't think you'd do it," Arrington replied.

I said, "Tell him thank you, but it's against the law."

The more I thought about that situation, the more I realized that if I had been gullible enough--or stupid enough--to accept that offer, I probably could indeed have gotten Carlile out of the race; but that lawyer who fixed the deal would have had me in a very bad situation from then on. "He would have had his foot on my neck," I confided to a friend.

My campaign got a major boost from an editorial that appeared in the *North Star*, a newspaper published in Britton, a northern suburb of Oklahoma City. The editor and publisher, Walter Harrison, had been among the military forces liberating the Philippines near the end of World War II at the time I was released from three years of incarceration at the Japanese prison at Bilibid, more dead than alive. While undergoing rehabilitation, I had the occasion to meet Harrison, then a colonel in the U.S. Army, who seemed greatly impressed with my story of escape and survival. Harrison offered to fly me back to the U.S. to speak at War Bond rallies, but I declined the invitation. Nevertheless, out of this experience Harrison and I formed a life-long friendship.[5]

The next day, I went by Harrison's office to thank him for the editorial. I told him how much I appreciated what he had done.

He volunteered a suggestion. "Do you know what I would do with it if I were running for office?"

"No, what?"

"I would have it reproduced and hand out a hundred thousand copies of that all up and down your district," he said.

"Do I have the newspaper's permission?" I asked.

"Yes you do."

Following Harrison's advice, my campaign staff distributed thousands of flyers containing reprints of the *North Star* editorial.

Then someone came up with the idea of taking out paid advertising space in the *Daily Oklahoman* and the *Oklahoma City Times* to run the editorial in the form of political advertising. But when they took the copy down to the newspapers, both papers refused to accept the ad. They explained that my opponent's name appeared in the ad and it was against the law to put the name of anyone in an advertisement without that person's permission.

Until then, I had not been aware of the law cited by the newspapers. It was not an election law, nor did it express any intent with regard to a political race. Rather, it was an obscure statute somewhere that applied to newspaper advertising.

That experience taught me a lesson. It is easy for politicians to run afoul of campaign laws. In good faith they may do something, unaware that it is unlawful. That is something candidates have to watch for at all times, because ignorance of the law is no excuse to violate it--particularly for a would-be supreme court justice.

Now I had another problem: thousands upon thousands of the flyers had already been printed and distributed throughout the eight-county area. They couldn't be recalled, so my all-volunteer staff did the next best thing, they spent hours and hours going through all of the remaining copies and striking off the name of Lon Carlile with a marking pen.

Curiously, the newspapers then agreed to carry the advertisement with my opponent's name marked out. It turned out that the ad was probably more effective in its revised form than it would have been had they left Carlile's name in it.

As the campaign wore on, more and more people came up to tell me about the horrible condition they thought the supreme court was in. More than one person implied that justice was for sale in this state.

For example, my good friend Jimmy Harden came to me and

said, "Bill, you shouldn't have entered this race."

"Why?" I asked.

Harden replied, "There are all kinds of crooks on that thing, and I just hope and pray that you won't get contaminated by them."

Now, we have to keep in mind that Jimmy Harden's dad was old John Harden, the man who built a lot of highways for the state of Oklahoma. Harden had amassed considerable sums of money and was a heavy financier of political races--including senators, governors, and members of the house. Rumor had it that he had bought and paid for a lot of legislation. Since Jimmy had been brought up in that kind of atmosphere, I figured he knew pretty well wherein he was speaking.

Harden was not alone in his opinion. A considerable number of lawyers also suspected the court was contaminated.

We sent out a questionnaire to the nearly 2,000 lawyers in Oklahoma County. It produced a tremendous response. We interpreted the response from the legal community as meaning that it wasn't merely that they thought me to be such a good lawyer or outstanding person; rather, they thought my track record as a county judge demonstrated that I was neither a captive of the entrenched powers nor would I be corrupted by them.

Many lawyers wanted to talk about the *Meadors* case. This was a case where a man's wife and a hired man had run off with all the children. The man, in due course, got divorced, married again, and started another family. Subsequently, he became very wealthy. When he died, his will left the first family out of the estate altogether. The first family came back and contested the will, and it eventually reached the supreme court. The general feeling among lawyers was that an injustice was done in the supreme court decision, which could only be explained by the speculation that certain lawyers had been able to exert their influence on the court.

Another case they wanted to bend my ear about involved an old school board decision in Oklahoma County decided many years before. One of the prominent lawyers of the time had gone to Brazil to keep from having to testify.

Also, there was an embarrassing situation involving Harlan Grimes, who had been on the losing side in the 1956 *Marshall v. Amos* case. Grimes loudly and publicly proclaimed that some supreme court justices had been bribed in connection with that case. He made such a nuisance of himself that he was eventually disbarred.[6]

As the campaign was nearing its end, I drove one day to the town of Watonga, west of Oklahoma City. I wanted to visit with Art Loewen, the town's mayor. Loewen was married to my cousin Virginia and also served as my campaign manager for that county.

Loewen ushered me in to see "Cowboy" Curtin, the publisher and editor of the Watonga *Republican*. Curtin reached into the top drawer of his desk and pulled out a cartoon drawn by the paper's political cartoonist. Handing it to me, he said, "I'm not going to publish this in the paper, but I do want you to have it."

The cartoon was devastating! It depicted the Supreme Court of Oklahoma in the hands of a puppeteer. Five puppets were controlled by one set of strings and the four others were standing to the side with puzzled looks on their faces.

The more I learned about the atmosphere and low repute of the state supreme court, the more it strengthened my resolve to get onto the court myself to become an influence for its betterment. To be sure, I would be only one person among nine and I realized I would have to bide my time until I got a little seniority. Somehow, I remained confident that one day the right opportunity would arise.

At the same time that I was running for the supreme court, Howard Edmondson--a "young man on the go"--was running for governor, having pulled off a stunning upset in the Democratic primary. He was young, energetic, very personable, reddish-blonde hair, and had a great speaking voice. Otis Sullivant, political writer for the *Oklahoma City Times*, described Edmondson as, "one of the most natural television personalities I have ever encountered." Edmondson came by his political talents naturally; his brother was a U.S. Congressman from Muskogee.

I ran into Howard on the campaign trail. He said to me, "Say, Bill, why don't you pick up some advertising on the television the day before the election? I'm going to take a big part, and why don't you take a big part of it so that my opponents and your opponents can't get on radio or television at that time?"

Well, I had been running public opinion polls on my own campaign, and they told me that I was running well ahead of Judge Carlile. I didn't want to spend as much money as television and radio advertising would have cost. So, I told Edmondson, "As far as I'm concerned, I'm running way ahead of my opponent and I don't want to spend that kind of money." That was all there was to that.

Edmondson went on to win the election, and he made a very fine governor. I had no political ties whatsoever to him. In fact, I disagreed with him on some important issues. Nevertheless, I felt he was one of the best governors we have had in this state.

I won the election over Lon Carlile by an astonishing two-to-one margin in all eight counties.

The next morning, one of Carlile's fellow justices asked him, "How are you feeling after the campaign?"

Carlile replied, "Do you know what? I got blitzed!"

In my opinion, Lon Carlile carried his defeat with grace and dignity. I was forced to acknowledge, "If that had been me, I wouldn't have been nearly as gracious a loser."

7

Trial by Senate

Not since the turbulent 1920s had Oklahoma conducted an impeachment trial. In 1928 the senate tried supreme court justice J. W. Clark. The vote in that trial fell one short of conviction. The following year Governor Henry Johnson was removed from office by impeachment. Now, 36 years later, the house and senate found themselves engaged in another impeachment proceeding--and with very little precedent to go on. Accordingly, house and senate members alike were burning the "midnight oil," poring over their law books, trying to figure out what to do.

State laws provided that the governor and other elective state officers, including justices of the supreme court, shall be liable and subject to impeachment for willful neglect of duty, corruption in office, habitual drunkenness, incompetency or any offense involving moral turpitude committed while in office.

An impeachment is defined as "the prosecution by the House of Representatives before the Senate." Articles of impeachment are formally the "written accusation of the officer, drawn up and approved by the House of Representatives."

* The articles of impeachment are drawn up and approved by the house and an impeachment is ordered;

* A board of managers shall be appointed by the house of its own members to prosecute;

* The chairman of the managers is directed to lay the articles of impeachment before the senate within five days;

* The senate is required within 10 days to organize as a court of impeachment;

* When this court is organized it is directed by law to "appoint a day for hearing the impeachment";

* The law gives the court of impeachment the power to make rules of procedure, to compel the attendance of witnesses and to punish for contempt;

* Before the senate considers the articles each senator is required to take this oath: "I do solemnly swear (or affirm) that I will faithfully and impartially try the impeachment...and do justice according to the law and the evidence";

* After the impeachment trial, the case is submitted to the senators and the roll is called on each article in open session;

* The law states, "if two-thirds of the senators present shall vote yes upon any charge or count contained in the articles of impeachment, the accused shall be adjudged guilty, and the judgment of the court shall be that he be removed from office."

Other language in the law says judgment of impeachment shall not extend beyond removal from office, "but this shall not prevent punishment of any such officer on charges growing out of the same matter by courts of the state."[1]

In the eyes of many people, Napoleon Bonaparte Johnson was as unlikely a candidate for impeachment proceedings as one could ever expect to see. His record of personal achievement topped that of almost any member who would be sitting in judgment over him. The *Oklahoma City Times* wrote of the 74-year-old justice:

"A Cherokee Indian, Justice Johnson was born in Maysville (Oklahoma) in 1891 and was reared in Claremore. He attended Tulsa University and received a law degree from Cumberland University, Birmingham, Alabama.

"Before his election to the state supreme court, he served 13 years as a district court judge in the state's 13th judicial district.

"He began his career in 1921 when he was employed in the probate department of the Osage Indian Agency of Pawhuska. He served as assistant county attorney in Rogers County from 1924 to

1930 and became city attorney in Claremore in 1932, a position he held until 1934.

"He was a member of the inter-tribal council of the Five Civilized Tribes and served as its president. He also was president of the National Congress of American Indians. He has served several years on the Governor's Interstate Indian Council and was reappointed in 1963 by Gov. Bellmon.

"He was named the outstanding American Indian in 1954, based on nominations from various tribal councils.

"He served as president of the National Hall of Fame for Famous American Indians at Anadarko and last June was named outstanding Indian of the year by the American Indian Exposition at Anadarko."[2]

On April 6, the senate organized as a court of impeachment and ordered Justice N. B. Johnson to appear at 2:00 p.m. the following Monday, April 12, 1965 to answer or plead to bribery charges filed by the House of Representatives. The suspended justice was served with the summons at his capitol office by the senate sergeant at arms, who was also elected marshal of the impeachment court.

As widely anticipated, Sen. Roy Grantham, Ponca City, was elected presiding judge of the court. Senate President Clem McSpadden, being from Johnson's judicial district, had appropriately disqualified himself.

In the eyes of his peers, Sen. Grantham was considered to be a "giant of a man," one who could be counted on not to let the trial become a three-ring circus. Blessed with a strong personality and astute legal mind, he was known throughout the area for his honesty and integrity. Before his election to the senate fifteen years earlier, he had served on the judge-advocate staff in the U.S. Army in Germany during World War II, and was the prosecutor in the army trial of the famed Hess crown jewels theft which sent two American officers to prison. With Grantham in the chair, Justice Johnson could be assured of receiving a fair trial before the Oklahoma state senate.

The senators stood, raised their right hand, and were sworn in as members of the court. They pledged to "faithfully and impartially try the impeachment against N. B. Johnson and do justice according to the law and the evidence."

Basil Wilson, the senate's secretary, was elected clerk of the court and Miss W. E. Shipley was elected journal clerk. Twenty-six assistant sergeants at arms were sworn in as assistant marshals for the trial.

The first fireworks were touched off when Sen. Don Baldwin, Anadarko, suggested that the press should be moved off the senate floor into the balcony for the trial. He said the press table might be needed by the accused and his attorneys. Other senators said they thought it very important to have the press close enough to hear the testimony and give an accurate report to the people. They argued that careful and complete coverage of the trial would be "of benefit for the people of Oklahoma."[5]

Baldwin retorted, "I don't think the accused and his attorneys should be forced into the galleries." The final decision was left to a special committee to handle seating arrangements.[6]

With its organization as a court complete and a trial date set, the senate then adjourned until 11:00 a.m. Thursday, when it would reconvene as a court to consider receipt of the summons on Johnson.

Justice Johnson engaged as his attorneys Fred Green of Sallisaw, and George A. Bingaman of Purcell. Bingaman was a former supreme court justice, having served one year on the high court during 1951-52 to fill a vacancy. Green had been prominent in Democratic politics for many years, former second district Democratic chairman and former member of the Democratic state executive committee. His son, Bruce Green, was the new U.S. Attorney for the eastern district in Muskogee, Oklahoma.

The suspended justice told reporters, "I want to have a full and complete hearing. The most important thing is to clear my name. I think the truth will finally prevail."[7] Those remarks squelched further speculation as to whether Johnson would resign or take his chances with the senate trial.

The senate met briefly on Thursday, April 8, as a court of impeachment to receive return of the service of summons served on Johnson by Frank Truel, court marshal. Sen. Grantham explained that Johnson's appearance on Monday would be similar to an arraignment in district court. He said it would be possible for the trial to begin immediately, but he indicated this was not likely. The court then adjourned until Monday.

Suspended Justice N. B. Johnson appeared before the senate, sitting as a court of impeachment, at 2:00 p.m. Monday, April 12, to enter his plea. Standing before the court with his attorneys beside him, Johnson said, "My plea is to plead not guilty. I want the public to have a true and complete hearing in this matter in order that the truth may be known."

His attorneys asked for a continuance until May 6. The prosecutors concurred, and presiding officer Roy Grantham set the trial to begin at 9:00 a.m., May 6. He said it was the court's intention to "begin and continue until trial is completed."[8] The senate would stay in session as court on Fridays and Saturdays. (Normally, the senate adjourns on Thursday.)

In one of the defense motions, Johnson's attorneys requested copies of the reports on N. S. Corn's medical and physical condition immediately prior to the time he was sentenced to the federal prison hospital. The motion also sought records while he was in the facility, a record of all Corn's visitors, and a record of all correspondence received by and concerning Corn. The defendant's motion contended that Corn "...was committed to the Springfield Hospital, which is a psychiatric institution. This on its face indicates that said N. S. Corn was undoubtedly at the time suffering from a substantial psychiatric disturbance."[9]

The prosecution objected, maintaining that the motion was "highly prejudicial."

On Thursday, May 6, 1965, trial began in the senate chambers, fourth floor, state capitol building, in Oklahoma City, Oklahoma. The senate was sitting as a court of impeachment.

Prosecution of the case was conducted by a Board of Managers appointed by the House of Representatives. Members were Rep. Lou S. Allard, Drumright; Rep. Burke G. Mordy, Ardmore; Rep. James W. Connor, Bartlesville; Rep. Phil Smalley, Norman; and Rep. Nathan S. Sherman, Oklahoma City. Connor was the sole Republican member.

Rep. G. T. Blankenship, as Republican house leader, had an opportunity to be on the prosecution team but declined to do so. Blankenship felt that inasmuch as it was he who brought the issue to the public's eye in the first place, it might appear to be vindictive on his part if he also served as prosecutor.

Johnson won the opening round of his ouster trial. The big test came as house prosecutors in their opening statement told the senate that they wanted permission to refer to five additional supreme court cases that were not mentioned in the impeachment articles.

Sen. Grantham ruled against the prosecutors and called for a 30-minute recess to allow senators time to read the offer of proof made by the prosecutors. At the end of the recess, the prosecutors appealed the ruling to a vote of the senate. They lost the appeal 27-19.

Rep. Connor told the senate that the five additional cases which they sought to interject into the prosecution would show "a conspiracy, if you will, between certain attorneys and certain officers of the supreme court."[10]

Arguing against the point of proof was Fred Green, attorney for Johnson, who said none of the five cases pointed to any guilt on Johnson's part.

The senate's rejection of the five cases meant that the prosecution would be narrowed to just the two cases which the house cited in its March 24 Articles of Impeachment.

Johnson's attorneys also sought to challenge the senate's jurisdiction to even hear the case. In a legal brief, they charged that the alleged bribes took place during a previous term of office by Johnson on the court. They argued that a public officer cannot be punished in one term for acts he committed in a previous term. On this matter, however, Johnson lost.

The first witness was Paul S. Copeland, branch manager of Brink's, Inc. Copeland identified his own records which established the fact that $125,000 was delivered to Hugh Carroll, president of the now defunct Selected Investments Corp. on April 24, 1957.

Hugh Carroll followed Copeland to the stand. In a dramatic story, Carroll told how he carried $150,000 in bribe money to former Justice N. S. Corn. Carroll's testimony came over the vigorous objections of Johnson's attorneys, who fought against Carroll telling how he paid the bribe to Corn.

In the first part of his testimony, Carroll told how founded Selected Investments Corp. and how suit was brought in 1954 by the Oklahoma Tax Commission to collect over a half a million dollars in taxes. Rep. Mordy asked him if the contention made by the Oklahoma Tax Commission was upheld, "what would it have done to Selected Investments Corporation?"

Carroll answered, "The Corporation Management Company would have been destroyed."

Under questioning, Mordy established that Carroll had known ex-Justice Corn since 1906.

Q. "Now, directing your attention specifically to the time that the *Selected Investments Corporation* case was before the supreme court, did you have an occasion to contact N. S. Corn at that time?"

A. "I called Justice Corn on the telephone and arranged to meet him over at his home, and we met and talked in my automobile and discussed the matter of the case coming up in the Court, and I outlined to him how important it was for us to have a decision in our favor."

Q. "Would you state, then, Mr. Carroll, what you told Judge Corn at that time?"

A. "The upshot of it was that we said that it meant $150,000 to us."

Q. "Did Judge Corn indicate to you that he understood the proposition?"

A. "He did."

At this point, the defense launched an unsuccessful attack against Carroll's testimony. George Bingaman objected that there was no evidence in the record at this time that the accused was in any way involved in a conspiracy with anyone, either Corn or Carroll. Presiding officer Grantham ruled against him, stating that the court is receiving this information into evidence with the understanding that it will later be linked.[11]

Under direct examination, Carroll testified that on April 10, 1957, he delivered $25,000 in one hundred dollar bills to Judge Corn as an advance payment on their agreement. He said he drew $23,000 from his personal account at First National Bank, and took the other $2,000 from his safety deposit box.

Q. "And you subsequently did what with the $25,000?"

A. "I gave it to Justice Corn."

Q. "Did you have any further communication with N. S. Corn?"

A. About two weeks later I had made arrangements with the First National Bank to have delivered to me $125,000 in hundred dollar bills, and after that money came into my possession, I called the judge and told him it was available...which was per our agreement. He came down to the office as he had before. I met him across the street and delivered the money...right south of the County Courthouse."[12]

Under intense cross-examination, defense attorney Bingaman sought to undermine Hugh Carroll's credibility. Bingaman questioned him intensely on his various business dealings, his involvement in a bank that went into receivership, the charges of fiscal mismanagement filed by the Oklahoma Securities Commission, his perjurious testimony at the bankruptcy proceedings of Selected Investments, and his conviction in federal court of 31 counts of defrauding investors. In essence, the defense was asking,

If you lied all those times in the past, why should we believe you now?

Following the afternoon recess, there were just a few more questions for Carroll. Perhaps the most interesting revelation came when Senator Grantham asked, "When you paid the $25,000 to N. S. Corn, what was it supposed to be used for according to your understanding with Judge Corn?"

Carroll answered, "There had been an indication that part of it was to be used for campaign expenses."

Lest the significance of this startling revelation be lost on the court, the house prosecutor, when his turn came again, zeroed in on Carroll's admission.

Q. "On a question by the Court, you stated that campaign expenses were mentioned to you. Campaign expenses for whom?"

A. "For the members of the Court."

Q. "And this information was given you by whom?"

A. "Mr. Corn."[13]

The final question to this witness was by the court. Just as Carroll was about to step down from the stand, the presiding officer asked, "Do you know to whom, meaning the members of the Court, the money was paid?"

A. "Outside of Justice Corn, I do not."[14]

That question and answer could not have been scripted better to set the stage for the prosecution's next witness.

8

Clash of Comrades

Two old comrades who once sat together on the state's highest court now squared off against each other in a different kind of court room. Former Justice N. S. Corn, 81, was on the witness stand in the state senate, and twenty feet away suspended Justice N. B. Johnson, 74, sat in the seat of the accused.

United Press reporter Alex Adwan described the scene for his readers: "Corn wore a coat, but no tie. His wrinkled gray shirt was open at the collar. A wisp of white hair lay uncombed across the top of his almost-bald head.

"Johnson, always a neat dresser, was impeccable in a gray suit that matched his thick, neatly combed hair."[1]

Corn glanced briefly at his old friend, then took a sip of water from a paper cup. Johnson's eyes never left Corn.

After a few preliminary questions by house prosecutors, Corn calmly told the senate he had received bribes for favorable court opinions in two cases and shared the money with Johnson and former Justice Earl Welch. Corn fumbled a few times with his hearing aid and sometimes cleared his throat, but his voice was firm and his testimony was clear.

He was asked to recite the circumstances involving the financial transactions in the *Selected Investments* case.

"Mr. Carroll, president of Selected Investments, he called me one morning and said he would like to take me out to Glen's to dinner that evening. He wanted to talk to me about something, so

I agreed to go. He arranged to come by my house about 6 or 6:30, pick me up, and on the way out there he mentioned this case. We went on out and had dinner and talked a little bit about it coming back. I think we finished up and we drove to my home where I live now. He said that he would give $150,000 to get a favorable opinion in this case.

Q. "Did you have occasion to visit with him several days later about this?"

A. "Well, a few days later after I had made an investigation I couldn't understand why he wanted to give that amount of money, so I wrote down on a sheet of paper in writing $150,000...and I called him and told him that I would like to see him. I made arrangements to drive down there south of the courthouse. He came across, got in the car, then I showed him this sheet of paper and told him I didn't want there to be any mistake about the amount, and I asked him if that writing was correct, a hundred and fifty thousand dollars, and he said it was. I don't recall anything else we talked about."

The house prosecutor then asked Corn what he did after this conversation.

"Well, I started out to make arrangements about getting enough members of the Court to give him a favorable opinion. I contacted two members of the Court."

Defense counsel objected when Corn was asked which two members. Objection was overruled.

Corn stated that the other two justices were Judge Johnson and Judge Welch.

The prosecutor then asked Corn to talk only about what took place between himself and Judge Johnson, leaving Judge Welch out of the discussion.

"Well, I told him I had a deal with Hugh Carroll and I had known Hugh Carroll for many years, he was president of a large concern and I thought he would be all right and I could get him $7,500 if he would go along with a favorable opinion." Corn said those may not have been his exact words, but in substance that is what he said.

Q. "Was anyone else present at the time of that conversation?"

A. "No, sir."

Q. "What did Judge Johnson say at that time?"

A. "Well, he said he would have to give it some thought. He didn't know whether an opinion could be written reversing it. But he talked like he would go along if it was possible."[2]

A few questions later, the prosecutor asked, "All right. What happened when the mandate came down in this particular case?"

Corn: "Well, it came down on Tuesday...I called Mr. Carroll on Monday, the day before, and told him I would like to see him, and I went down. I think this was right after noon when I went down. I told him the mandate was coming down the next day. We discussed it awhile. He wasn't prepared, he said, to take care of it. And I asked him if he could make a payment as much as $25,000, and he said yes, he could make that payment, get it out of his personal account, I believe. And said it would take him a few hours to do that, so I told him I would come back to the Capitol Building and then he could call me when he got ready to go on it. So when I got back to the Capitol Building, I got in touch with Judge Johnson and told him to stay at his office that evening.... I told him to stay in his office until I reported to him."

Corn recounted how he picked up the money. "So later on I got in touch with Carroll...I don't know whether he called me or I called him, said 'Everything is okay,' and I drove down there south of the courthouse. He came across, got in the car, and put the $25,000 in the glove compartment of my car, in the place up there. I drove around a block or two and let him out. I came back to the office here, and I counted out $7,500. This was all in $100 bills, and I got in touch with Judge Johnson, went to his office, gave him $7,500 and told him to count it out, and he counted it out. That's about all there was to it."

Q. "Did you also deliver the same amount to Judge Welch?"

A. "Yes, sir, the same amount."

Q. "Did you notice if Judge Johnson counted the money when you gave it to him?"

A. "Yes, I stood there, and he counted it."

Q. "Was there anyone else present at the time that you gave him the money?"

A. "No, sir, nobody else was present."[3]

Corn rarely looked in the direction of his old friend. He seemed preoccupied with his handkerchief, his hearing aid and the microphone that often seemed too high or too low.

Johnson's mouth was drawn from tension, but his expression never changed during the testimony of his former colleague.

The house prosecutor next directed Corn's attention to the case involving *Oklahoma Company v. O'Neil*. The ex-justice told a similar story of receiving cash and passing it on to Welch and Johnson for a favorable ruling in an oil lease lawsuit.

"What brought this case to your attention?" the prosecutor asked.

Corn: "Mr. O. A. Cargill called me, wanted me to come out to his place where he was living northwest one Saturday afternoon, he wanted to talk to me. So I went out there, and he got in my car.... He told me that he had a case up here that he had to get reversed, said it involved his daughter and son-in-law, and I think he mentioned that there was a criminal action at that time or would be one filed against his son-in-law and his daughter in Florida. And he wanted to know whether he could get it reversed. He said he would give $7,500 to Judge Welch, Judge Johnson, and me, if we could get that case reversed. And he wanted to know if I would take it up with them. He said, 'You are up there handy,' and he said, 'I've got some of the other boys to see.' And I told him I would. And I did."

Q. "What did you do after your conversation with Mr. Cargill?"

A. "Well, I contacted...Judge Welch and Judge Johnson, told them the deal with Cargill."

Q. "Did you contact them together or separately?"

A. "No separately, I never did talk with them together about anything wrong."

Q. "What did you discuss with Judge Johnson at the time you talked to him?"

A. "I told him about Cargill had a case and his daughter was involved and he wanted it reversed, and I thought we ought to reverse it for him if we could, and told him the deal, that he would get $2,500 out of it. He said he would go along if he could, he didn't know just what the facts would be."[4]

In a series of questions that followed, the prosecutor established that Corn delivered the money to Johnson in his office, that Johnson counted out the money in front of him, and that nobody else was present at the time.

The cross-examination of Justice Corn was conducted by defense attorney Bingaman. The first part was marked by the attempt to ask a series of questions regarding the condition of his health at various times in the past--apparently with the intent to discredit the ex-justice by casting doubt on his physical and mental competence. The prosecution objected and was sustained by the presiding judge. Bingaman, however, was persistent.

Bingaman: "If I could be heard one moment on it, if the Court please. The purpose of asking the question is to establish to the Court here, to have some idea of his present physical condition, and his physical background as to his competency as a witness."

Presiding Officer: "Perhaps there might be some other questions admissible in this regard, but I believe they are improper. The objection will be sustained."

Bingaman: "May I ask him as to his health at the moment?"

Presiding Officer: "You may."

Q (By Mr. Bingaman). "I observe, Judge Corn, that there is a sore on the side of your face. Would you know what that is?"

A. "Well, the doctor said it was a skin cancer. I've had it removed and it's healing up now."

Q. "A few days since I was in your home and you were showing me sores on your leg...."

Representative Mordy: "I am going to object again, Your Honor; completely irrelevant, immaterial, to the questions he is asking."

Presiding Officer: "The objection is sustained. You can go to the question of his competency as a witness, but I don't believe you are doing that, and the objection is sustained."[5]

Thus thwarted in its attempt to establish physical and mental incompetence, the defense then turned to trying to find inconsistencies in testimony that Corn had previously given to various investigative authorities in the past. The day ended with procedural wrangling between house prosecutors and defense attorneys.[6]

Before adjournment, the Court posed a question of its own. "Did you advise Mr. Carroll the name or names of any other judge or judges whom payment was to be made in the *Selected* Case?"

A. "I did not."

When testimony resumed on Friday morning, ex-Justice N. S. Corn was back on the stand, wearing a dress shirt and necktie.

Reporter Bob McMillan of the *Oklahoma City Times* wrote: "Stripped of all but his dignity and never wavering in his testimony, former Supreme Court Justice N. S. Corn looked downward on the senate court of impeachment Friday like a judge from the bench.... One could almost visualize the former justice still in his office as he casually said he took a $150,000 bribe and gave part to his colleagues but kept the lion's share for himself."[7]

The reporter added, "For 24 years, former Justice Corn represented the people of Oklahoma in their court of last resort. It seemed incongruous to hear testimony from a man of such bearing."[8]

It became evident early in Friday's hearing that Justice Johnson's attorneys were not going to be very successful in discrediting Corn's testimony. The ex-justice would not be stampeded into hasty answers. Occasionally, he would ask that a question be repeated, but generally his answers were direct and not evasive.

Cross-examination questions brought statements that he did not tell Johnson or Welch he had received $150,000 as a bribe for the *Selected* case. It was also brought out that he had trouble with the late Justice Ben Arnold, who once slapped him while attending a conference. However, he said he had no ill feelings toward Arnold.

Not even the defense's final cross-examination question could shake the old justice's aplomb. "I will ask you Judge Corn, if there was ever a single year that you served in the 24 years on the supreme court that you didn't take money to influence your vote in cases there?"

The presiding officer overruled the question, but not before Corn had replied in part, "I had arrangements...."[9]

When asked, on redirect examination, why he only gave $7,500 each to two of his colleagues out of the $150,000 bribe he received, Corn caused a loud titter from the audience when he calmly replied: "That was an arbitrary amount that I fixed...I just wanted to keep the rest of it, I guess." [10]

Laughter turned to disgust a few moments later when it was revealed that the name of a fourth justice was linked to the bribe in the *Selected* case. This testimony came after wrangling among the senators, in which the senate overruled its presiding officer.

The prosecutor asked, "Judge, of the $25,000 you received on April 10, 1957, did you do anything with any of that money other than $15,000 which you have testified about?"

A. "Yes, sir, I gave $2,500 to O. A. Cargill."

Q: "For what purpose, Judge?"

A. "To get.... "

Objection by defense counsel to this line of questioning was sustained by the presiding officer.

Frustrated by the unwillingness of the presiding officer to allow questions along this line from either the prosecutors or members of the senate, Sen. Cleeta John Rogers called for a vote of the senate. Grantham explained, "The reason I am holding as I am...is that the charges under the Articles of Impeachment involve these two cases only, and I am excluding testimony as to any other possible cases."

Sen. Bryce Baggett argued: "There has been presented by the

Board of Managers the question of a common plan, scheme and conspiracy. The question, if addressed to that particular element of the case, would be material within the two Articles."

By a vote of 22 to 24, the chair was overruled and questioning was allowed to continue.[1]

Q. "Did you have any type of agreement in regard to the vote of Judge Carlile in the *Selected Investments* case?" (Carlile, now deceased, left the bench in 1958 after his defeat by me.)

A. "Yes, sir."

Q. "With whom did you have an arrangement in regard to the Carlile vote?"

A. "O. A. Cargill."

Q. "What was that arrangement?"

A. "I delivered $2,500."

A. "How did Judge Carlile vote in the *Selected Investments* case?"

A. "He concurred in the opinion."[12]

Further questions by house prosecutors and members of the senate impeachment court sought to learn why Corn thought he could buy Welch's and Johnson's votes. Each time the question was asked, Corn would reply that his reason for approaching the two justices was based on hearsay.

Q. "Tell the court why you believed that you could approach...Judge Welch and Judge Johnson in this matter?"

A. "I didn't know they would, as far as that goes, for sure. I figured they would from what I observed."

Q. "What had you observed, what did you know?"

A. "Along in '55 or the first of '56..."

An objection by Johnson's lawyers that Corn was about to utter some hearsay testimony was upheld by the presiding officer. House prosecutors argued their contention that Corn's answer would constitute an exception to the general rule because they had established a conspiracy. "Your honor," argued Rep. Mordy, "it is our contention that Judge Corn did a particular act because of knowledge that he had. This knowledge is predicated on something he was told. It is a contention of the Board of

Managers that this goes into the very reason that an act was done, and whether or not it is predicated on hearsay, it is an admissible question."[13]

Johnson's attorneys argued that there was not one word about a conspiracy in the impeachment articles in the house. These articles simply charged Johnson received $7,500 to vote a certain way in one case, $2,500 to vote in another case.

Presiding officer Grantham ruled Corn could not answer the question if it involved hearsay testimony. The house prosecutors appealed his ruling to the senate. This time, members of the senate sustained their presiding officer and that line of inquiry was blocked. That ruling not withstanding, persistent prosecutors were able to phrase their questions in such a way as to elicit from Corn testimony to the effect that his opinion regarding Welch and Johnson had been based on the prior case of *Marshall v. Amos.*[14]

In earlier testimony, Sen. Finis Smith, Tulsa, wanted to know, "What prompted you to make these disclosures after so many years?"

Corn replied, "I didn't think it would ever be brought out. I didn't think Hugh Carroll would ever disclose it.... I made up my mind that I never was going to tell anybody anything about this deal unless I was forced to. If it ever came to a place where I would have to take the witness stand and testify, I was going to tell the truth. I wasn't going to tell a lie for anybody."[15]

Corn was followed to the stand on Friday afternoon by a California housewife, Mrs. Roscoe D. Farmer. A former Oklahoma City resident, Mrs. Farmer testified to a conversation she had with Harold Westcott, son-in-law of O. A. Cargill, Sr.

Mrs. Farmer testified that Westcott, one of the parties in the *Oklahoma Company v. O'Neil* case, wanted to sell her an oil and gas lease during the time that the case was on appeal in the Oklahoma Supreme Court.

Q. "Mrs. Farmer, what reason did Harold Westcott give to you and Mr. Farmer for attempting to sell this oil and gas lease?"

A. "He told us that he had to pay off these judges to get out of this indictment.''

Q. ''Did he name the judges?''

A. ''Yes, he did.''

Q. ''What judges did he name?''

A. ''Johnson, Welch and Carlile.''

Cross-examination served only to bring out further damaging testimony. Mrs. Farmer testified to an attempted ''shakedown'' by people who worked for O. A. Cargill, Sr. Johnson's attorneys asked her if she believed that ''all of us lawyers are practically crooks?''

''Well, so far I have found them that way,'' Mrs. Farmer answered.

Q. ''Do you think all judges are crooks?''

A. ''So far....''[16]

The white-haired, bespeckled Justice Johnson, on trial for his political life, bore a serious expression throughout most of Mrs. Farmer's testimony. Occasionally, he smiled weakly when his attorneys seemed to make a point.

The galleries were almost full, with some seats taken by law students who hurriedly scribbled down bits of testimony for future reference. Senate secretaries, accustomed to being off on Fridays, had to work, and used their spare time to sit in the galleries. Rep. Allard, surveying the numbers, said, ''We're making a little bit of history.''

The prosecution wound up its testimony on Friday with introduction of Johnson's bank records. Monty Williams, vice president of First National Bank of Claremore, identified records of Johnson's checking account and savings account. He said the primary source of the checking account was monthly salary checks. He said the savings account had been closed January 16, 1956. He did not testify as to the amount of money in either account.

He was followed by Kenneth Lawton, cashier of the Citizens National Bank in Oklahoma City, who identified 36 cashier's checks that Johnson had purchased from July 26, 1956 to March

3, 1962 that totaled $6,099.89.

Earlier, prosecutors read into the record the fact that Johnson's salary since 1961 had been $16,500 per year, and from 1951 through 1960 it had been $12,500.

When the hearing resumed on Saturday morning, May 8, the only witness presented by the house prosecutors was Kenneth Lawton, whom they recalled briefly for additional testimony. Lawton was asked his opinion as to whether the safety deposit box registered to Justice Johnson was capable of holding $7,500 in $100 bills. He assured the court that the box could easily hold that amount.

With that, the prosecution rested. Now it would be Johnson's turn.

9

The Power of One

The defense, which had previously delayed its opening statement until now, took the floor. Attorney Fred Green opened the defense with a blistering attack on Justice Corn.

"If it please the Court, we are going to show you a contrast. You have already seen from that witness chair an evil old man. A man who admits he has lived a life of corruption.

"We are going to show to this Court a different kind of man. We are going to show you a man, seventy-four years of age, who has lived a life that his family, his children, his friends and his neighbors can be proud about....

"We are going to show you where N. B. Johnson was born in the State of Oklahoma down in the southern part of the state...that he is part Cherokee Indian and in his early life he left that part and went back to his native territory in the Cherokee Nation....

"We are going to show you further honors that this man has gained throughout his lifetime. The confidence that his friends and neighbors and the people of this state have placed in him. Instead of showing you a life of corruption, we are going to show you a life of honesty, a life of integrity, a life that he in his old age can look back upon and be thankful that he himself never accepted a bribe to change or get his decision in any case.

"Of course we are going to put him on the witness stand. He is going to tell this Court and this Court is going to believe him when they hear him. I truly believe that N. S. Corn falsely testified from the witness stand when he said that N. B. Johnson accepted $7,500 from him in the *Selected Investments* case or $2,500 from him in the *Oklahoma Company* case.

"We will also show you the reputation and kind of man that N. B. Johnson is and compare him to N. S. Corn. As you will see from the witness stand, he is not going to be the kind of a man that can sit there and look out over this audience, look at his two sons sitting up in the gallery, and say, 'Yeah, I took a bribe.' 'Yes, I don't remember a year that I have been on the supreme court that I didn't take a bribe'--with all of the confidence, not one single bit of remorse. When you hear this man testify, hear him, you are going to know that N. B. Johnson didn't do the things he is charged with in this case."[1]

Green's opening statement was followed by a group of character witnesses, including two district judges and two justices of the supreme court, Denver Davison and Chief Justice Harry L. S. Halley.

Chief Justice Halley said he knew Johnson as a law-abiding and truthful citizen. The same question was asked of, and the same answer given by, C. F. Bliss of Tahlequah and Claude Garrett of Fort Gibson, both district judges.

W. E. McIntosh, Tulsa County treasurer and principal chief of the Creek Indian tribe declared Johnson--half Cherokee and once-named American Indian of the Year--"a credit to our nation."

Rep. James Connor, one of the house prosecutors, reminded McIntosh that resigned Justice Earl Welch is also part Indian. "Are you also proud of him?" Connor asked.

"I am proud of any Indian," McIntosh said.

Justice Davison was questioned about the court opinions in the two cases involved in the impeachment charges. He said he concurred in both opinions.

Q. "In Case 36731, *Selected Investment Corp. v. Oklahoma Tax Commission*...did you, at the time you joined in this opinion, believe it was good law and in accordance with the former decisions of the Court and precedents?''

A. ''I thought so.''

Q. ''The other case brought in issue here is Case No. 38178, entitled *The Oklahoma Company v. O'Neil.* Was it your belief at the time you joined in that opinion that it was a good opinion and pronounced the law as you found it at the time in the State of Oklahoma?''

A. ''I thought it was a very close case, but I thought it was correct."[2]

Members of the senate had a series of questions to ask Davison. ''Did you observe any unusual activities by any justices in connection with the two cases?''

''No, sir, I did not.''

''Were you contacted by Justice Johnson or any other person to influence your vote in either the *Selected Investments* or the *Oklahoma Company* case?''

''No, sir. The only...the only...only in the conference room, we always discussed these cases in conference quite in length, but I was never talked to by Judge Johnson on either one of these cases outside the conference room.''

Davison added, ''It's not unusual for us to disagree on opinions."[3]

In an effort to counter the defense's picture of Justice Corn as an ''evil old man,'' and despite vigorous objections from Johnson's attorneys, the prosecution managed to elicit from Justice Davison essentially the same statement he had previously made about Justice Johnson, namely, ''I can't recall any time when I had any suspicion of Judge Corn accepting any bribe.''

Earlier, Johnson's attorneys had approached me--as, I assume, they did all justices--about testifying as a character witness for him. I told the attorneys, ''Yes, I will be a character witness, but I'm going to tell the truth. I'm not going to stretch anything. Personally, I don't really think that Johnson was taking money, but I do think he was capable of being easily influenced.''

Johnson's attorneys never called me to the stand.

Other people who did testify as character witnesses for Johnson included Wheeler Mayo, Sallisaw publisher; Joe McBride, Anadarko publisher; District Judge Tom R. Blaine, Enid; Amos Ward, Claremore, Rogers County sheriff; and District Judge John Q. Adams, Vinita.

A whimsical sidebar article was written by Leonard Jackson in Saturday's *Oklahoma City Times*. Headlined, "Court Podiums Stir Comment by Lawyers," Jackson wrote:

"Six pieces of furniture that quietly served their purpose for several years at the courthouse have become the subject of conversation.

"They're podiums at which lawyers stand to argue their cases in Oklahoma County district courtrooms.

"What makes them the center of attention is the presence on each of a small metal plaque reading: 'Donated by O. A. Cargill.'

"Some city lawyers have protested what they consider an unfair advertising advantage to the influential attorney.

"The comment has become especially caustic since Cargill was indicted in both federal and state courts in connection with alleged bribery of some state supreme court justices.

"The judges are understood to be perplexed by the suggestion of impropriety in the presence of the plaque-bearing podiums.

"'We've probably had them 10 or 15 years,' said one. 'Nothing was ever said about them until the last few months'."[4]

Opening his defense on Monday, May 11,. Johnson branded the testimony of former Justice Corn as "absolutely false."

His attorney Fred Green asked him, "Did Justice Corn pay you a bribe of $7,500?

"He did not," Johnson replied with heat in his voice.

Green then asked him if he had ever received a bribe in the *Oklahoma v. O'Neil* case. Once again, Johnson replied with vigor that he had not, repeating that the testimony was false.

Johnson also testified that he had done nothing to conceal tax information from the federal authorities. He said his tax return was investigated by the Internal Revenue Service in 1959 and

1960 and that a letter from Earl Wiseman, former district director of internal revenue, confirms this.

In a surprise move--perhaps hoping the impeachment court would take it easy on him--Johnson said he intended to retire from the court and become a supernumerary justice at the end of his present term in 1967. He said he made the decision after he was re-elected in 1960. "I felt like thirty years on the Bench active was enough," he told the senators.

If Johnson thought he would have an easy time of it, that thought was lost on the house prosecutors. They gave him a thorough going-over.

Early in the cross-examination, a very damaging admission was drawn out of Johnson. It came in response to questions by one of the prosecution team, Rep. James Connor. Connor baited the trap by asking Johnson whether he thought it would be improper for a legislator to approach a judge about a case.

Johnson said, "I think it would be improper to approach any judge."

Then Connor sprung his trap. "Judge Johnson, have you made telephone calls to various friends of yours around the state of Oklahoma asking them to intercede in your behalf among members of this court?"

Johnson was forced to admit that he had talked to some friends, but he insisted that all he wanted was to receive a fair deal.

Connor pressed home the point: "Did you feel it necessary, sir, to contact the members and insure you received a fair deal?"

"No, I didn't," a chastened Johnson replied. He also said he could not recall how many telephone calls he had made.[5]

The prosecutors then turned to the main task at hand, that of weaving a financial web around the embattled justice. First, they established that Johnson had opened a safety deposit box at Citizen's National Bank in Oklahoma City on June 10, 1957, shortly after the alleged payment of $7,500 was made in the *Selected* case. Prosecutors seemed interested in the timing of this transaction, considering the fact that throughout the previous 10 years since moving from Claremore, Johnson had not had a safety deposit box.

"I wouldn't know at this time," Johnson said.

Also, the justice was unable to offer a satisfactory explanation as to why his wife's name was not on the register when her name was on all of their other bank accounts as joint tenant. "I didn't know that she couldn't get in there," was the reply.

Under the hammering cross-examination, Johnson attempted to explain purchases of almost $7,000 in 36 cashier's checks from 1957 to 1962. The prosecution brought out that most of the checks were purchased on the same days that he visited his safety deposit box at the bank.

When asked where he got the money for these cashier's checks, the veteran justice told the court that he had a hoard of hidden cash that he kept at his house.

Q. "How much do you usually keep there, sir?"

A. "I had about fifteen hundred or two thousand dollars."

Q. "And where did this money come from, sir?"

A. "Accumulative withdrawals, I drew from forty-five to fifty dollars, maybe twice a week here in the Treasurer's Office."[6]

When asked where he kept the money at his house, Johnson insisted he stored it in his bedroom over the window top, "right over the top of the curtain on the window in my bedroom." He said he did not keep a written record of the amount of money he had at home.

Later in the questioning concerning his frequent entries into the safety deposit box, Johnson said he had put $800 in the box on one occasion. The prosecutors pointed out that several of the cashier's checks were made payable to Johnson's account in the Claremore bank.

The prosecutor summarized that Johnson testified the money originally came from his Claremore bank account and he was in fact returning money previously withdrawn. Asked why such a practice was followed, Johnson said he did not want the total accumulated withdrawals to become too large.

The prosecution pointed out that apparently Johnson had ceased using cashier's checks to pay his household bills after March 3, 1962. They also brought out that on April 12, 1962, attorney Harlan Grimes had written Johnson accusing him of taking a bribe in the *Selected Investments* case.

Q. "Can you give us a reason why after Harlan Grimes confronted you with the bribe taking in the *Selected Investments* case, sir, you stopped giving cashier's checks?

A. "No, I don't have any reason to offer."[7]

Johnson also testified to receiving more than $3,500 in campaign contributions in 1959 and 1960, even though he did not face any opposition. He said he considered the donations as "trust funds" and when he did not receive an opponent he could either use the money or return it to the contributors.

Asked what he did with the money, Johnson replied, "I retained it all." Asked whether taxes were paid on the money, he answered, "No, I didn't know whether it is taxable or not."

When asked where he deposited the money, Johnson said he kept it in his fund "up over the window."

Court adjourned at 5:30 p.m. to resume again on Tuesday.

In his second day of testimony, Justice Johnson said he felt that the man who accused him of taking $10,000 in bribe money did it to cover up his own corruption. The 74-year-old justice said former Justice N. S. Corn "had to make some explanation, I guess, as to what he was going to do with the money. He had to have an excuse for flimflamming someone (out of $150,000), I imagine."

House prosecutors introduced the savings accounts records of Johnson and his wife, Martha. They were prepared to test his testimony that he juggled between various savings accounts to explain how he deposited more money in them than his supreme court salary.

Sens. Ted Findeiss and Richard Stansberry asked Johnson how in the period January 1, 1956 to January 1, 1965, he could deposit in the bank $11,500 more than he received as salary as a supreme court justice. Johnson gave a convoluted answer:

"Well, I just don't remember, but what I usually did, if I ran short on my checking account I would borrow money from the Claremore Federal Savings & Loan and deposit that money in my First National Bank account, and I borrowed money from the Claremore Building & Loan on different occasions. Then I borrowed some from the Local Federal Savings & Loan, and I deposited that, but I don't recall. I have an auditor that's gone into all of that and for all of the years involved, that is, the years '57 through '64, but I can't remember those details, but I am quite sure that the source from which those deposits came were from other accounts. When I would run short in my checking account at First National Bank, I would borrow from other sources. And sometimes I would receive expense checks. For instance, I went to...when I was on the Governor's Interstate Indian Council, I made trips, sometimes that would amount to $100 or $200 or more. I think I deposited some of that in the Claremore bank, but most of those checks were in the building and loan, but that's the best answer I could give to that question right now." [8]

Sen. J. Lee Keels then asked Johnson how he could account for the approximately $20,000 of deposits more than his payroll checks during the last four years, 1961 to 1965.

"I don't...I couldn't give an intelligent answer to that without consulting the record. I just don't know. I'm sure I could explain it, but I wouldn't want to attempt to right now because I don't have the data before me."[9]

Sen. Charles Pope said that Johnson's records indicate he spent $5,000 more from 1957 to 1961 than he received in salary from the state.

"Well, again, we ran into accounting, but I think when you have examined my net worth statements from '57 to 1961...you will find, taking into consideration my income and my contributions...you will find that I am well within my income for the period."[10]

Whenever house prosecutors questioned Johnson in detail about his personal finances, his answer often was "I don't know" or "I don't remember." Reporter Hugh Hall of the *Oklahoma City*

Times kept a running tally. In a little over six hours of testimony Monday and Tuesday, Johnson answered "I don't know" 17 times and "I don't recall" or "I don't remember" a total of 58 times.[11]

The notion of racism was injected into the proceedings by Sen. John Young of Sapulpa. "Do you feel that Corn holds any ill will against you because you are an Indian?"

"Well, I am an Indian, and a fellow he had a fight with and his wife was an Indian, and Welch was an Indian. I just don't know. I never tried to inject that into any campaign or anything, but there could have been a deep-seated prejudice there, but I have nothing on which to base it."[12]

The *New York Times* was quick to pick up on the racism theme. Next morning's edition trumpeted "Anti-Indian Bias Hinted by Judge." Reporter Donald Jansen wrote, "Justice Napoleon Bonaparte Johnson of the Oklahoma Supreme Court suggested today that anti-Indian prejudice might account for bribery charges against him." The article suggested that beyond prejudice, there was no other reason for Corn to implicate Johnson.[13]

Johnson left the stand shortly after 11:30 a.m., only to be called back briefly for a few additional questions by the prosecution. The prosecution then called to the stand three witnesses, two from savings and loan associations and the third from an Oklahoma City bank, to describe Johnson's deposits in those institutions.

The impeachment trial struggled slowly through a jungle of financial figures Tuesday afternoon. Orval Veirs, Oklahoma City attorney and accountant, presented a detailed report of the income and expenditures of Johnson, all designed to show that the accused justice had no hidden sources of income from January, 1957, through the year 1963.

Veirs said the statement had been prepared and presented to federal tax authorities and in his opinion Johnson had made full payment of all taxes due.

Veirs' report--compiled from bank records, tax returns and Johnson's statements--showed Johnson depositing all of his state salary checks in his Claremore bank and then writing checks each week to obtain cash for spending money. Under the defense theory, this would explain where Johnson obtained the cash to purchase $6,909.89 worth of cashier's checks from July 26, 1956 to March 3, 1962.

Johnson's defense suffered a severe setback on Wednesday, May 12, however, when the accused justice's tax expert, Orval Veirs, was forced to retreat on some of his statements. The prosecution tore heavily into his previous day's testimony throughout the morning hours.

Under withering cross-examination from Rep. James Connor, Veirs admitted that it "was a valid assumption" that Johnson had spent more money than was available to him. Veirs was forced to admit:

1. that it was impossible for him to account for all of Johnson's expenditures;
2. that a financial statement he introduced on Tuesday didn't include all of Johnson's spending over a five-year period; and
3. that a statement made in court Tuesday was incorrect.

Veirs asked the court for time to study his financial table. "There seems to be something wrong with adding the net worth," Veirs said.

Presiding officer Grantham then called the noon recess so that Veirs might study the prosecution's contentions.

When questioning resumed, life did not get any easier for Veirs. Veirs was asked by Connor if his financial statement told whether Johnson reported on his income tax all that he spent.

"No, it would be impossible," Veirs replied, "because I have no way of telling what he spent in cash."

As Connor continued to quiz the expert, Veirs admitted that the figures he listed on the non-deductible expenditures were incorrect. He said such a table had been prepared for submission to the Internal Revenue Service.

"Then many of your figures are incorrect for the purpose of this court?" Connor demanded.

Veirs admitted that they were.

Connor then reminded Veirs of testimony he made on Tuesday. "You answered, 'In my opinion it proves that he has made a full report of his income, because he has reported and paid taxes on more money than he spent.' Was that statement correct then?" Connor inquired.

"It was not correct," Veirs replied.

One member of the senate asked Veirs to explain a $7,902 discrepancy over a two-year period in his report when Johnson withdrew from his bank more than he spent in 1960 and spent more than he withdrew the following year.

"I cannot explain it," Veirs answered.[14]

Senators fidgeted in their chairs, puffed nervously on cigarettes, or stared at the defendant as attorneys from both sides made closing arguments. His hands folded on his lap, Justice Johnson sat impassively throughout the last moments of his historic trial.[15]

Prosecutors, in their final arguments, said their principal witness, former Justice N. S. Corn, 81 and in ill health, was looking his maker in the eye when he said he shared $157,500 with Johnson. Rep. Lou Allard, chairman of the five-man prosecution team, moved to defend Corn as a witness even before Corn was attacked by defense lawyers. "He was 81 years old," Allard said, "and getting ready to meet his maker. He wanted to do something right...in order that he may go to his maker."[16]

Opening for the defense argument, attorney George Bingaman pounded hard at what he said was the prosecution's failure to back up its witness charging bribery. Bingaman also sought to undermine confidence in Corn as a witness.

"We learned long ago from Hitler and fellows like him that if you're going to tell a lie, you'd better tell a big one." Bingaman said. "They say this man (Corn) is contrite...and did you see anything contrite about him?"

Bingaman then asked the senate to consider why Corn would accuse Johnson. "Why would Corn do this sort of thing?" Bingaman questioned. "He said he was a man of arrangement, that he made them every year he sat on the supreme court bench."

"And in making this statement while still in prison, he made an arrangement for immunity," Bingaman asserted, "...and the victim was poor Nap Johnson."[17]

The senators started their deliberations at 1:28 p.m. They deliberated behind closed doors before taking a roll call vote in open session. It would take a two-thirds vote--32 out of the 47 present--for conviction. If found guilty, Johnson would be ousted from the bench.

At 4:37 p.m. the senate came back into open session with the attendance roll call.

"The court is now ready to vote on whether or not the court will sustain the articles of impeachment," intoned presiding officer Roy Grantham.

Johnson sat facing the senate and darted glances at a roll call sheet his attorneys were keeping. Separate roll calls were taken on each article.

It was a moment of tense drama as clerk Basil Wilson began the historic roll call. There was not a sound from the chamber or from the partially-filled galleries, other than the recording of the Aye and No votes.

"Atkinson?" the clerk called. "Aye."

"Baggett?" "Aye."

"Baldwin?" "No."

"Bartlett?" "Aye."

"Berrong?" "Aye."

"Berry?" "No."

"Birdsong?" "Aye."

"Boecher?" "Aye."

"Bradley?" "Aye."

"Dacus?" "Aye."

"Field?" "Aye."

"Findeiss?" "Aye."

"Garrett?" "Aye."

"Garrison?" "Aye."

"Gee?" "Aye."
"Grantham?" "Aye."
"Graves?" "Aye."
"Ham?" "No."
"Hamilton?" "Aye."
"Holden?" "Aye."
"Horn?" "Aye."
"Howard?" "Aye."
"Keels?" "Aye."
"Luton?" "Aye."
"McClendon?" "No."
"McSpadden?" "No."
"Martin?" "Yes."
"Massad?" "Yes."
"Massey?" "No."
"Miller?" "Aye."
"Muldrow?" "No."
"Murphy?" "Yes."
"Nichols?" "No."
"Payne?" "No."
"Pope?" "No."
"Porter?" "No."
"Rhoades?" "Yes."
"Rogers?" "Yes."
"Romang?" "No."
"Selman?" "Yes."
"Smith?" "Yes."
"Stansberry?" "Yes."
"Stipe?" "No."
"Taliaferro?" "No."
"Terrill?" "Yes."
"Williams?" "Yes."
"Young?" (Pause)

The count stood at 31 yes, 15 no, one short of conviction. The full weight of responsibility now fell upon the shoulders of one man, Senator John W. Young of Sapulpa. His vote, "Aye" or

"Nay" would spell the difference between conviction and acquittal. He felt the air so thick that he could almost cut it in front of him. Running through his mind was the fact that he had taken Johnson's figures to his own accountant, and the judge's figures did not add up. Yet, he hated to vote guilty because he had always liked the man.[18]

The clerk repeated the call:

"Young?" "Yes."

The clerk then announced the vote, 32 Ayes and 15 Nays. In a solemn voice weighted with sadness, the presiding officer declared:

"Two thirds of this court having voted Aye, I declare Article One to be sustained and you are thereby under the constitution and statues found guilty and it is the judgment of the court that you be removed from office as justice of the Supreme Court of Oklahoma."

Johnson sat at the front of the senate, stunned, his hands still folded in his lap and his head inclined downward. He became the first supreme court justice in Oklahoma's history to be removed from office by impeachment.

Grantham pronounced the same judgment after Article Two was sustained. Then he declared the court adjourned.

There were no slaps on the back or victorious cheers. It was a sad day for Oklahoma. The senators walked the capitol rotunda with misty eyes. A few Johnson supporters clustered around him, including Sen. Clem McSpadden, President Pro-tempore, from Johnson's home town, Claremore. None of the senators looked at each other. They were looking out in space or straight ahead.

Johnson walked to meet the press on the senate floor. He read a one paragraph statement and then distributed copies.

"While I am deeply disappointed with this verdict, I am glad to have had the opportunity to give the people of Oklahoma my side of the story that they may be the final judge."[19]

The former justice left the chamber and descended a capitol stairway accompanied by members of his family.

Former Oklahoma Supreme Court Justice N. S. Corn testifies in the impeachment trial of another justice, N. B. Johnson. Copyright, 1965, Oklahoma Publishing Company. From May 7, 1965 issue of *The Daily Oklahoman*.

Justice Earl Welch arrives at the Oklahoma house chambers Tuesday, March 9, 1865, for a hearing on bribery charges. Copyright, 1965, Oklahoma Publishing Company. From March 10, 1965 issue of *The Daily Oklahoman*.

Oklahoma Supreme Court Justice N. B. Johnson listens intently to the verdict in the trial which ended in his disgrace and removal from the bench. Copyright, 1965, Oklahoma Publishing Company. From May 14, 1965 issue of *The Daily Oklahoman*.

Rep. Burke G. Mordy was chief counsel for the House Investigating Committee that recommended impeachment of Justice N. B. Johnson and Justice Earl Welch, who resigned before trial. Mordy was also principle author of the ''Mordy Plan'' of court reform.

Rep. G. T. Blankenship reviews stacks of paperwork in the state house chambers. Copyright, 1965, Oklahoma Publishing Company. From January 21, 1965 issue of *The Daily Oklahoman*.

Hugh A. Carroll (r), former president of Selected Investments Corp., is charged with fraud. Copyright, 1958, Oklahoma Publishing Company. From May, 10, 1958 issue of *The Daily Oklahoman*.

Flanked by members of his family, O. A. Cargill Sr. leaves the federal courthouse after being convicted on three counts of perjury. Copyright, 1965, Oklahoma Publishing Company. From June 16, 1965 issue of *The Daily Oklahoman*.

House Speaker J. D. McCarty, the uncrowned 'king' of the Oklahoma legislature, was convicted in July 1967 of two counts of income tax evasion and sentenced to three years in federal prison. Copyright, 1965, Oklahoma Publishing Company. From January 21, 1965 issue of *The Daily Oklahoman*.

Publisher of the Watonga *Republican* gave this unpublished cartoon to William A. Berry during Berry's 1958 campaign for election to the supreme court.

Justice William A. Berry (l.) takes the oath for his fourth term as justice of the Oklahoma Supreme Court. With him are Justices Pat Irwin and Don Barnes.

10

Politics of Influence

(A Short Course in Judicial Ethics)

A rational motive can always be given by a judge who sells his honor and his decision. The testimony of both Justices Welch and Johnson makes it clear that, in his own mind, a corrupt judge can always offer a rationalization for the abasement of his office and oath.

There is no complete explanation of what makes a judge corrupt. Some judges move through their office without ever a hint of taint or impropriety. Others move more like a figure in a Greek tragedy, inexorably along the path toward self-destruction.

Nor is there a discernible type of corrupt judge. You can't recognize one walking down the street. Justice Corn admitted that there was never a year in his 24 years on the court when he did not take a bribe. On the other hand, no judge ever fell from such a pinnacle of respectability or so fully betrayed his early promise as did Justice Johnson.

A part of the answer lies in the enormous amount of pressure that is placed on the judge. This pressure comes from a variety of sources, including friends, business associates, civic leaders, artful lawyers, fellow judges, state legislators, and even the governor's office. As one cynic put it, "When the pressures on both sides are equal, then you get judicial fairness."

As a result, the judge's life is not an easy one. The Canons of

Judicial Ethics of the American Bar Association require that the judge's personal behavior "in his everyday life must be beyond reproach." <Canon 4> He often foregoes many of the indulgences and pleasures permitted ordinary people. His friends and associates must be chosen with great care. In essence, the Canons thus impose upon the judge the degree of propriety as that expressed in the "Caesar's wife" doctrine.[1]

My wife doesn't like me to tell this story, but for a long time whenever she received a traffic ticket I would say to her, "Just give me the ticket and I'll take care of it." Then I would simply write a personal check to pay the amount due, not realizing that she mistakenly assumed I was having the ticket "fixed." It all came to light one evening at a dinner party when a guest casually mentioned that he got a traffic citation on the way to the party. Whereupon, my wife said, "Oh, just give it to the judge, he'll take care of it. After all, that's what friends are for."

In its homespun way, that story points to something that can be a major problem for judges, namely, the attitude--*that's what friends are for*. That attitude, widely held by the general public, creates almost as much grief for judges as anything else they do.

Social Relationships

Friendship is a highly prized commodity. Aristotle, in his *Ethics*, wrote, "Without friends, no one would choose to live, though he had all other goods."[2]

Yet, this same friendship can become a liability if it creates the impression of partiality or bias. The concept of equal justice is meaningless if some parties benefit from a relationship with a judge, while others do not. Because of this, most judges bend over backwards to avoid the appearance of favoritism or partiality by *recusing*, or disqualifying, themselves when a friend or associate appears in their court.

It is very difficult for many people to understand why a judge who is his friend would ever come down with a decision that would be against that individual. Naturally, they always think the facts of the case are on their side and that any fair-minded person would see that they are in the right. Therefore, it comes as a shock and a disappointment when the case goes against them, and they feel let down by their friend.

For example, my wife's grandfather, the legendary Dr. G. A. Nichols, a very prominent builder in early Oklahoma City, was hurt and offended when his friend, Supreme Court Justice R. A. Hefner, sat out a case that involved Nichols. The two men had been very close friends for many years, went on trips together, hunted together, entertained socially. Not only that, their wives were best friends also.

"Doc" Nichols, as he was generally known, had a case come before the supreme court pertaining to a dispute over some land development he was involved in. Judge Hefner, who was looked upon as one of the outstanding, honest judges, disqualified himself from the case. It was the only thing he could do honorably and ethically because of his friendship with Nichols.

Many years later, Nichols told this story to me. Even at such a late date, it still rankled him. He simply could not understand why his old friend had deserted him at a time when he could have helped. Nichols saw it as a matter of honor and trust, saying, "For some reason, I just can't trust him because he wouldn't stay on that case."

Oddly enough, I myself had experienced a somewhat similar incident when I was still a young man in college. A classmate's father was a justice on the Oklahoma Supreme Court and whenever I passed through Oklahoma City, I made it a practice to stop in and visit the judge in his chambers. The old judge would always express pleasure at seeing me and would offer me encouragement along my life's path. It happened that while still in college, I was found negligent in an automobile accident, and the settlement ended up on appeal before the supreme court. Not knowing any better, I couldn't wait to visit my friend on the supreme court and tell him every aspect of the case. Later, when the opinion came down, I won on a technicality but I was shocked to discover that my friend, the judge, had disqualified himself in the case and had not participated.

Professional Relationships

Professional friendships can also be a source of pressure. Some judges avoid the opportunity for pressure by routinely disqualifying themselves from proceedings in which former associates from their law offices are involved.

Shortly after I joined the supreme court, I was contacted by a former law partner, at that time a district judge, whose son-in-law was involved in a closely-contested race for a seat in the state House of Representatives. As a matter of fact, this race was so close that at the end there had to be a recount. Certain ballots in it had been challenged, and these ballots would make the difference in the outcome. Whether or not they were judged to be legal ballots would determine who won or lost the race.

The whole matter ended up in the lap of the supreme court. At the time it was set for vote in conference, I was scheduled to attend a judicial assembly in Santa Fe, New Mexico. However, I had already decided I did not wish to participate in this case, so I went ahead and made the trip. The decision of the majority of the court was that these ballots were good votes, which meant that my former partner's son-in-law lost that election. (In later years, that son-in-law did get elected to the House of Representatives and subsequently became Speaker of the House.)

Ever after, whenever I would run into my former law partner, I couldn't help but notice a definite air of coolness on his part. Clearly, he bore a resentment that I didn't do as he thought I should have done, namely, to have stayed on the case. But for my part, I didn't feel I could rule on the case without some kind of feeling one way or another. My motto was that "a judge could have no friends or no enemies."

Some time later, an old friend of both of us wrote me a letter and let me know in no uncertain terms that I was not a friend after all, that I had done something very bad by sitting out that particular case, and as a consequence the judge's son-in-law had lost the election because I had turned his back on a friend. I was sorry he felt that way about it, and I wrote him a long letter in reply explaining that under the code of judicial ethics I felt I shouldn't take part in the case.

Those things do happen; and they tear at the fabric of friendship, loyalty, and bonds between a judge and his friends.

Artful Attorneys

The Code of Judicial Conduct provides that, except as authorized by law, judges may "neither initiate nor consider *ex parte* or other communications concerning a pending or impending proceeding."[3] *Ex parte* communications are defined as those which involve discussion between the judge and only one side of the matter. Such one-sided communication is deemed improper because it presents only one side of the argument and deprives the absent party the right to be heard and to respond.

Most attorneys are too smart to approach a judge head-on to engage in *ex parte* communications. More likely, they will employ a more artful or subtle means.

One such tactic was tried against me at the time I was sworn in as justice of the supreme court in January 1959. I returned to my new chambers after the swearing-in ceremony and found a large basket of flowers waiting there for me. Naturally, I looked at the card to see who they were from, and the card indicated that the flowers were from a local attorney, whom I shall refer to as "John Doe." I knew Mr. Doe to be a bond attorney of considerable reputation, although I was not personally very well acquainted with him. The card simply congratulated me on my office and wished me well.

About a week later, Mr. Doe called me, saying, "I understand you have been assigned such-and-such case, and I would like to come out and go over a procedure with you about a special matter."

"Why sure," I said. "Come on out."

When Mr. Doe arrived in the chambers, he closed the door behind him, fingered his hat, and sat across the desk from me. "Justice Berry," he began, "I have filed an original jurisdiction here--a case which I hope the supreme court will consider--and I would like to talk to you about the procedure." Since this was a type of case that I had not been involved in previously--either as a lawyer or a county judge--I said I was glad to get the information. Mr. Doe then went on to explain how the supreme court might reach down into one of the lower courts and either stop the action, or ask certain questions that might save an appeal later.

Pretty soon, however, Mr. Doe started talking about the other side, what dirty so-and-sos they were, and how they were playing all these dirty tricks on him. I stopped him right there. "Wait just a minute Mr. Doe. You came out here to discuss procedure, which was great, and I appreciate it. But now you're getting into the merits of this lawsuit."

With that, Mr. Doe stood up, glared at me, took his hat and rotated the brim of it a couple of times, glared at me again, then turned and stalked out, slamming the door behind him as he left. Because the door was a big, heavy door, it slammed rather hard.

A few days later, I received a letter from Mr. Doe. The letter said he didn't mean to upset me, but he was only doing what he had been doing for many years...going out and discussing matters at the court. There had never been any objection to it, and he just couldn't understand my attitude because of other judges who had let him do it.

Nevertheless, I couldn't help noticing that Mr. Doe's letter didn't contain the slightest hint of an apology. Rather, he was telling me what the facts of life were.

A second tactic some lawyers try is to find out which way a judge is leaning in a particular case. In this situation, the aim is not so much to pump information *into* the judge as it is to pump information *out* of him. Typically, the situation will happen like this: The artful attorney will approach the judge at a judicial conference, a bar association, a luncheon, a party, or any other place where judges and lawyers might bump into each other. Then, engaging the judge in casual conversation, the attorney might say, "You know, I have a case out there...." If the judge isn't careful, pretty soon the lawyer will extract the information he seeks.

The reason attorneys would like to know which way the court is leaning, is that it gives them a chance to go out and settle the case if they are about to lose the lawsuit. Or, conversely, if they find out they're about to win the lawsuit, it may help them to hold out for a stronger settlement.

I suspect this may have happened in a case involving Justice N. B. Johnson. Johnson's opinion had been rejected in conference by a vote of five to four and it was reassigned to me. When the case came back for rehearing, Johnson kept stalling and stalling and stalling, saying to the other judges, "If you will just give this a little more time, I think the parties are about to get a settlement worked out."

At the time these delays were going on, none of us inferred that Johnson had an *ex parte* communication with the losing side. However, in the light of his subsequent impeachment, some of us began to wonder if perhaps Johnson might have been trying to do a friend a favor.

A third tactic used by some lawyers is "name dropping." In this situation, the lawyer does not himself have any influence on the court, but he wants people to *think* that he does.

Early in my tenure on the court, one of the older justices told me about a situation that had occurred some years earlier. A certain lawyer was hauled before the bar association on a charge of violating professional conduct. It was alleged that he had represented to a client that he could control five members of the supreme court and if the client were to retain his services he could win the case because of his influence on the court.

In the hearing before the bar committee, this lawyer admitted that, yes, he did make that statement. But he went on to say, "I didn't mean it; it really wasn't true." He tried to explain that he was just trying to get the client to hire him in the case, and he thought he could improve his chances of getting hired if the client thought he really did exercise that much influence on the judges of the supreme court.

Regardless of what manner of confidential information is

obtained, whether it comes from a secretary, a legal assistant, a scrap of paper from the waste basket, a janitor, or someone who got into a judge's office and peeked at certain papers, that confidential information could be used by an artful lawyer to represent that he had knowledge. For example, if an unscrupulous lawyer were to learn that five judges were ready to concur in an opinion, one way or another, he could then go to a gullible client and claim that he exercised influence over certain judges--and could even name which judges.

Business Relationships

Since judges, as a rule, come to the bench following successful careers in law and business, they often bring with them certain business and financial interests. While theoretically it might seem like a good idea to require judges to divest themselves of all financial interests, on a practical level this is not a workable idea. At a very minimum, it might impose severe economic losses on those who take the bench.

Canon 5C(1) of the Code of Judicial Conduct recognizes this fact, and it states:

A judge should refrain from financial and business dealings that tend to reflect adversely on his impartiality, interfere with the proper performance of his judicial duties, exploit his judicial position, or involve him in frequent transactions with lawyers or persons likely to come before the court on which he serves."[4]

Business relationships do not always involve a direct conflict of interest. Sometimes the pressures can be more subtle. As an illustration of this, I owned some city lots in Oklahoma City, which I had purchased back in the late 1940s when I was a practicing attorney before I became a county judge. The lots, though platted, did not have street access. Twenty years later while I was on the supreme court, word filtered through to me that the city was planning to extend the streets in that area, which, if true, would mean that at long last I could develop that piece of property.

Late one evening, I got a telephone call from my friend Dan

Stuart who had part ownership with me in that property. Stuart reported, "A certain friend of ours, one of your good supporters on the supreme court, called me and told me that he had received a call from an unnamed individual down at the city. The gist of that call was that unless you vote a certain way on a case which the city has before the court, that street is not going to be put through to our property as had been planned and as we have been led to believe--that is, unless you vote in a certain way."

I was aghast at the naked threat. The case before the court had nothing whatever to do with our piece of property; the city was using that as leverage to twist my arm. I said, "Dan, even if I wanted to, now I wouldn't go that direction. I couldn't do it."

When it came time for the justices to vote in conference, I didn't go along. And although the case did go through the court on its merits, it did so without my help or participation. In my mind the attempted interference in the case did it a lot of harm and it did color my judgment.

Sometime later, still being wrought up about the situation, I was at a reception where I ran into the person whom I thought was the instigator, a respected civic leader. I confronted him about the issue and told him straight out, "I want you to know that my voting situation and my business situation have no connection whatsoever. The court is completely independent of any business affair that I may be dealing with."

The gentleman was rather startled by my outburst and vigorously denied any knowledge of what I was talking about. Then I realized perhaps I might have made a mistake, that perhaps this man was not the source after all; and indeed it was probably poor judgment to have confronted this individual in this fashion. Nevertheless, the good side of the story is the message began to spread that people shouldn't ever try to use business relationships to influence my vote.

In short, here was a situation in which as a judge I had no financial or business interest in the case before the court. I would not have benefited from its outcome. And so, under the Judicial Code of Conduct, I would not have been required to step aside.

However, because certain unscrupulous individuals sought to apply leverage, i.e., "You do this for me and I'll do that for you," the situation was thereby transformed into a conflict of interest; and I did the only honorable thing I could do, which was to take myself off the case.

Civic Activities

A regular visitor to the judges' chambers was Stanley Draper who, for many years, was the executive secretary of the Chamber of Commerce and a very powerful figure. Draper would come out to the court and usually bring some important person with him. "Now, Judge Beery," he'd say (he always pronounced my name as 'Beery'), "we're not out here to influence you...." And then he would go on with his spiel which, of course, demonstrated that he *did* want to influence the court.

Draper usually brought some little Chamber-of-Commerce type gift--a ruler, a note pad, a little memento of some trifling value. Whereas judges wouldn't accept anything from lawyers or litigants, they thought nothing of accepting Draper's token gifts because they had no monetary value.

"Judge Beery," Draper would typically say, "we've got a case out here that we're *highly* interested in. Now, all we want you to do--*all* we want you to do is see if you can't expedite it."

Generally, I did not take offense; I took Draper at his word, then went on to vote my conscience. But, of course, there was never any doubt as to which side of the question Draper was interested in winning.

Almost all judges have been active in public affairs. Not surprisingly, most continue to be interested and concerned about public events. Even though there is a broad public consensus in support of the judge's community involvement, it is not easy to maintain the appearance of impartiality when there is a policy conflict.

The *Atoka Water* case,[5] which came before the Oklahoma Supreme Court in 1960 was one in which there was a lot of civic pressure brought to bear on the court's decision. A bond issue of

$65,000,000 was involved.

This was a city trust. The city of Oklahoma City was trying to build a new reservoir for water in order to service the future growth and expansion of the city.

The supreme court's action was stalled for a long time. One of the sticking points was the form in which the trust was first presented to the court, namely, that a certain bank would have control of the trust through the appointment of directors. Justice Irwin and I, in studying the briefs and going through the articles of the trust, determined that, in fact, one bank would end up in control of everything.

Somehow or other, the word leaked out that certain members of the court were unhappy with this proposed arrangement. Subsequently, in a public meeting, the president of a rival bank created a ruckus when he stated, in effect, that he didn't think it was right for one bank to be in control. In his view, the city should have control of the trust, rather than a single bank.

Also in attendance at this meeting was E. K. Gaylord, publisher of the city's two main newspapers. When the newspaper speaks, the courts tend to listen. The consensus view was that Mr. Gaylord, on almost all occasions, had the community's interest at heart. Mr. Gaylord wanted this dam to be built and he didn't want anything to stand in the way of it. And from his point of view, this banker was just throwing a monkey wrench into the machinery, that he was someone stopping progress, and therefore he was an obstacle that had to be removed.

Eventually, the trust was approved and the Atoka Dam was built. But as finally approved, the city had control of the trust rather than the aforesaid bank.

State Legislature

In all probability, the state legislature is the body that exercises the greatest amount of pressure on supreme court judges.

Oklahoma's constitution, following the U.S. Constitution, created three branches of government with a series of checks and balances. The legislature creates the law; the governor, with his right to veto, administers the law as set forth by the legislature; and the courts are there to protect the people.

The courts protect the legislature from the governor, or the governor from the legislature. But primarily, the courts exist to adjudicate problems that arise with people against each other and to make certain that the government itself does not unduly impose upon the rights of individual citizens.

Theoretically, these three branches of government are supposed to be separate, distinct and equal; and it takes all three of them to conduct business. Despite the concept of "separation of powers," however, the state legislature nevertheless wields a heavy hammer over the judicial heads.

That legislative hammer is the power of the purse strings. The judiciary is completely dependent upon the will and the caprice of the legislative branch for its salaries, budget, number of judgeships, and jurisdictional boundaries. This control gives the legislature the power to punish and reward.

To understand this, a person needs to understand that the legislature and the judiciary operate by different sets of rules. The legislature normally works by the lobbying method. "You do a favor for me, and I'll do a favor for you." The legislators were used to constituents coming to see them. They were used to lobbying groups wining and dining them. They were used to special interest groups applying pressure. They saw nothing wrong with it; that's the way the legislature had always functioned; that's the way it was expected to function.

These being the rules of the game, the typical legislator felt little hesitancy in trying to influence judicial opinion. Not always did it involve heavy-handed arm-twisting; more often, the pressures were applied a little more subtly.

For example, suppose the legislature had before it some matters related to the creation of highways, issuance of tax-free bonds, or other pending legislation that might involve constitutional questions. In their zeal to get these things approved, individual legislators often felt little restraint on pressuring the supreme court to conform to what they wanted. After all, that was their natural way of doing business.

This attempt to lobby judicial opinion was often difficult for a judge to accept. It ran contrary to judicial ethics. Judges must be impartial both in appearance and in fact and undue pressure from legislators threatens the public perception of impartiality.

Therefore, while it may have been true that the judiciary was a separate and equal branch of government, it was at the same time wholly dependent upon the will and the caprice of the legislature for its budget, judicial salaries, and certain jurisdictional matters. As a case in point, there was no constitutional limitation to the number of courts of appeal or judgeships that could be set up--or eliminated--by the legislature. At such times as a matter of great importance to the legislature was before the supreme court, other matters of great importance to the judiciary might be bottled up in legislative committees. And while no spoken threat might ever be made, the judiciary nevertheless was always aware of that heavy hammer wielded by the legislature.

Unfortunately, economic conditions sometimes play a role in the sorry spectacle of judicial corruption. For example, when I joined the supreme court in 1959, my annual salary was $12,500, which was only $300 more than my salary as a county judge. When one considered the extra effort, the cost of mounting a campaign, and everything else that went with the job, the office of supreme court justice was a financial negative. Moreover, at the time the scandals took place, the state did not have a retirement plan for its supreme court justices. Only a short time before it had established a supernumerary relationship whereby a retired judge--under certain circumstances--might continue to serve the court and receive a pittance of income.

Coupled with this, supreme court justices were expected to maintain a respectable public image, not necessarily one of affluence but certainly one of dignity. Accordingly, salaries were very important to a judge. And who controlled the salaries? The state legislature, of course!

Be that as it may, I must hasten to affirm that not once during my almost 20 years on the court did I hear an individual senator or member of the house make overt threats about cutting the salaries of the supreme court. But on the other hand, there was always an awareness that the salaries of the justices were completely dependent upon the will, the whim or caprice of the legislature. It was amazing to me to see how school teachers and government workers could have their lobby groups out there working the halls of the capitol, while the poor, old supreme court justices, if they knew some legislator, could only say, "Please, increase our salaries."

When I was chief justice in 1971 and 1972, I prevailed upon the legislature to allow myself, as chief justice, to bring a "State of the Judiciary" address. One of the first things I said in this address was that the salaries of the supreme court and the judiciary as a whole should be increased. Afterwards, I was amazed at the number of judges who came up to me and stated how embarrassed they were that the chief justice should bring up such a touchy subject as salaries in his State of the Judiciary address.

Individual members of the legislature are not above using the prerogatives of office to gain their way. It has happened! Take a situation, for example, where a member of the state senate, a lawyer, may have a case before the supreme court which is very urgent to him. It may pertain to a fee which is tied up in the case. Suppose this senator, a long-time member of the legislature, highly regarded, highly respected, had important committees which he chaired, were to call up a justice and say, "I'm going out to such-and-such a judicial conference, could I drive you out there?" Somewhere along the way, he would happen to refer to this case he had in the supreme court, and usually it would have something to do with the winning or losing, but the whole point being that his fee, one way or another, might be involved completely in that case, whether he won or lost.

Well, he would start out on how hard up he was...how much he needed the money, and how much this fee, if he lost the case, would mean to him. That case would be such and such, and so and so, what was involved in it and how righteous his cause was.

And he might even shed a tear or two. Yes, senators have been known to go that far. To be sure, this is not saying that the senator would offer a bribe; but he is applying pressure and influence.

But then sometime along in the evening, on the ride there or the ride back, it might be brought up that there was certain legislation pertaining to the court pending in the senate--it might be about salaries, a jurisdictional question, operating budget, or perhaps something else very important to the court--but, in any event, the legislator would know how that judge felt and that his vote might be the swing vote. And then this lawyer-senator would bring out the idea how much time he had been trying to convince the members of the committee that he wanted them to recommend that legislation to the floor, and how he was working on it, and how he would continue to work on it. He might even throw in that judges need a raise in salaries. All these things would have an influence.

And, of course, the inference might be made that those doors would be closed completely in the future as far as this senator and the courts were concerned, unless that senator's case prevailed.

This kind of situation happened to me one time. Trapped inside the car, I had little choice but to listen. Moreover, I didn't want to insult my host. But the way I handled it gained me very little admiration or love from the senator; namely, when the matter came before the court I refused to vote on it--even refused to participate in the deliberations in conference as to decide which way the court should go on the case.

The end result is that I lost my "in," and I lost whatever friendship, whatever good feeling, I might have had with this senator. And ever afterward, the door to this particular senator's office was closed to me.

Executive Branch

Governors are not above trying to influence the supreme court in order to get their programs adopted. One such incident came to light after I had retired from the court in 1979.

Howard Edmondson, former governor, then U.S. Senator, spoke with me about the possibility of our forming a legal partnership when he left the Senate. Edmondson had been elected governor the same year that I was elected to the supreme court, and, of course, we knew each other very well. During the course of our conversations about forming a law office, Edmondson related an incident that happened during his governorship in which he tried to influence my vote.

It seems that at the time, Governor Edmondson was very interested in getting approval to issue some revenue bonds which would be used to extend the turnpike system from Tulsa eastward to the Missouri border.[6] The plan was to use revenues from the existing Turner Turnpike to subsidize and pay for the construction of the additional turnpike. However, there was some question as to whether the charter of the Oklahoma Turnpike Authority would permit this to happen. As initially conceived, the Turner Turnpike was designed to run between Tulsa and Oklahoma City, and once the bonds were paid off the tolls were to be discontinued and the road would revert to being a free Oklahoma highway.

I was not sure the state had a constitutional right to do this. In effect, the state would be taking property away from the people of Oklahoma. Moreover, under this rubric, the state could continue to build turnpike after turnpike, using money from roads that had already been paid out and thus extend *ad infinitum* the date when roads long since paid for would become public highways.

There was a big meeting in Tulsa to deal with the issue. High level leaders from all across the state were called to attend. Edmondson himself was in charge of the meeting.

During this high level strategy session, the name of each supreme court justice was called out. Whoever could get close to, or had an "in," with any of the court justices was urged to talk to the judge and exercise his or her influence towards getting a favorable decision. One such person was assigned to me.

I was completely unaware of this attempt to pressure me and it certainly did not have any influence on my vote. Although the bond issue was approved by a majority of the court, I had cast a "concurring in the results" vote which meant I did not adopt the opinion but I did want the turnpike to be built.

National Political Figures

Every once in a while, the state courts get caught up in a situation where a national political figure is involved. Such was a case involving a company controlled by Lyndon Johnson, then U.S. Senate Majority leader and, arguably, one of the most powerful figures in America.

The case involved the 1959 sale of television station KXII-TV located at Ardmore, Oklahoma, to a buyer in Texas.[7] Buyers and sellers jointly applied to the Federal Communications Commission (FCC) for approval of the sale and for a permit to transfer the television station to a new and more desirable location in Dexter, Texas. The contract contained an option clause that would expire on April 1, 1959, unless extended in writing and signed by both parties.

But when the application came before the FCC, it just bogged down. Another TV station in Texas protested the sale and the FCC refused to move. In due time, the option ran out and the parties orally agreed to an extension. On the day they were supposed to sign the papers, the seller backed out and refused to sign the extension previously agreed to. That same day, the FCC approved the application. Three hours later, the sellers executed a contract for the sale of the station to the Texas group.

The trial court threw out the case without hearing any evidence. The matter came before the Oklahoma Supreme Court charging that the sellers "connived and conspired" with the Texas group to avoid carrying out the terms of the contract. The supreme court unanimously reversed the lower court and reinstated the caue.

I was the one who wrote the majority opinion for the court. In my original draft, I identified Lyndon Johnson's company as being the real purchaser of the Ardmore station. However, in conference, one of the other justices suggested it would be prudent to delete the name of Lyndon Johnson--who by that time was vice president of the U.S.--from the opinion. I agreed to this deletion, inasmuch as it was not critical to the case.

After the opinion was published in the bar journal, the lawyers involved in both sides came to my office and asked, "Judge, we have worked this out. We've settled it, and everybody's happy. But we would all like that opinion withdrawn. Do you mind withdrawing it?"

I replied, "No, I don't mind withdrawing it. I am not here for the pride of authorship. I'm here to settle lawsuits." Nevertheless, in my mind, this incident illustrated the way politics can enter into judicial influence.

11

Focusing on the Fixer

A judge cannot be corrupt alone. For every corrupt judge, there are inevitable corrupters. Since January, people speculated as to who the shadowy "Mr. X" might be whom Rep. G. T. Blankenship alluded to in his speech on the floor of the House of Representatives. Allegedly, this Mr. X had a financial arrangement with Justice N. S. Corn for almost 20 years, whereby Corn would vote with the majority of the court in all cases where the unnamed lawyer was involved.

The perjury trial of Oklahoma City attorney O. A. Cargill, Sr., whom many people believed to be Mr. X, began in federal court on Tuesday, June 1, 1965. U.S. District Judge Roy W. Harper was the same judge who presided over the grand jury which indicted Justices Corn and Welch for federal income tax evasion and also presided over the trial of Welch.

Harper had been recognized as one of the most able federal judges in the U.S., having the distinction of receiving more appointments to the bench than any other judge. "It's what's inside the black robe that counts," he once told a new appointee to the bench. He also said that "nothing teaches a man how to be a good judge. His only preparation is to have been a fine enough lawyer to match any attorney who may stand before him in his court."[1]

Representing Cargill as chief counsel was flamboyant Houston attorney Percy Foreman. At age 60, Foreman was known throughout the southwest as a master of courtroom strategy and had been defense counsel in more than 700 murder cases. At one time, the Houston attorney was retained to defend Jack Ruby, convicted slayer of the accused presidential assassin, Lee Harvey Oswald; however, he pulled out of the Ruby case following disagreements with members of the slayer's family.

Assisting Foreman were Jack Grant Day, Cleveland, Ohio, and George Miskovsky, Oklahoma City. Day, age 51, had taught law at three Ohio colleges and was a specialist in trial work and constitutional law. Miskovsky, a long-time state Senator, had just two weeks previously cast his vote against the impeachment of former Justice N. B. Johnson. Also at the defense table were attorneys O. A. "Buck" Cargill, Jr., David Cargill, and John Chiaf, son, grandson, and law partner, respectively, of the accused.

Handling the prosecution was U.S. Attorney B. Andrew Potter, recently reappointed to a second four-year term in that office. Assisting him was David A. Kline, an assistant U.S. Attorney and former law clerk to the late U.S. District Judge W. R. Wallace. Also at the government's table was assistant U.S. Attorney John Raley, serving as escort for the government's witnesses.

O. A. Cargill, age 80, towering, craggy, gruff, was one of the most successful lawyers in the history of Oklahoma. Since 1912, when "Big Boy" Cargill patrolled the downtown streets as a city policeman, he had been a man on the way up. He had been mayor of Oklahoma City, Oklahoma County Attorney, candidate for governor, and a leader of the bar. In his youth, Cargill had been a steer roper in rodeos. In addition, Cargill taught Sunday school classes and was a deacon in the Baptist Church.

Others in the courtroom included Olive Poole, Judge Harper's court reporter from St. Louis; Doug Sanders, member of the federal court clerk's staff; Barritt Galloway, bailiff; Sandy Miller, Judge Harper's law clerk; and Miss Vera Howard, U.S. District Court clerk in Oklahoma City.

The jury of ten men and two women, plus two alternates, was

sequestered for the duration of the trial at the Skirvin Hotel--something not done in Oklahoma City's federal court in fifteen years. They were staying, each in a private room, on the same floor of the Skirvin, where the entire floor was reserved for them. Radio and television newscasts and newspaper stories of the trial were prohibited. They were also unable to receive telephone calls and the press was barred from taking photographs of the jurors. Around-the-clock guards kept watch on the floor even when the jury was at the courthouse. Judge Harper said that never before in his long judicial career had he felt it necessary to take such extreme precautions.

In a rare and unexpected move, Judge Harper secretly switched jury lists just three minutes before jury selection was set to begin. Unsuspecting jurors waiting patiently near Judge Fred A. Daughtery's courtroom, ready to go to work on routine cases, were instead led into Judge Harper's courtroom when the time came.

The sudden switch was made as a precautionary measure so as not to "take any chances" that the jurors might have been tampered with before the trial. Harper said the original jury panel, whose names had been drawn approximately ten days earlier, had been investigated by defense attorneys as to background, age, length of schooling, employment, number of children, and church affiliation, among other things. Thus, the trial began with a brand new list of 100 names.[2]

Cargill was charged with three counts of perjury. Count one charged that he lied to the grand jury with regard to his knowledge of the payment of $150,000 by Hugh Carroll to ex-Justice N. S. Corn in the *Selected Investments* case. The grand jury also charged that Cargill had received part of the money.

Count two dealt with the fictional personage Pierre Laval, about whom Cargill had denied any knowledge. The grand jurors alleged that Cargill created the non-existent Laval.

Count three of the indictment alleged that Cargill lied to the grand jury when he denied that he had ever had any financial transactions with any justices of the Oklahoma Supreme Court. The government charged that Cargill had "on a number of occasions" paid certain amounts of money to a member or members of the supreme court "to obtain favorable court rulings."[3]

In early legal maneuvering, Cargill's defense attorney, Percy Foreman, sought to postpone the trial. "The defense is not ready, your honor," he told the judge. Foreman pleaded for a trial delay because he said two key defense witnesses were "seriously ill."

Foreman named Oklahoma City attorney Ned Looney as gravely ill and unable to give testimony for at least 30 days. He also said impeached Justice N. B. Johnson suffered a relapse of a heart condition four days after his impeachment and had since developed a viral infection.

Reached later at her home, Mrs. Johnson denied that her husband had had a heart attack. "He is ill and in bed and not feeling well," she said, "but he certainly doesn't have a heart condition."[4]

Judge Harper sat impassively as Foreman spoke of his own health failing and other matters that he said would warrant a trial continuance. "I have always known I'll probably pass away in a court room and it might well be here and now," the Houston attorney told Judge Harper. He added that he did not expect to die soon, "but I do not believe my physical condition is such that I can effectively represent my client."[5]

But the noted attorney had met his match in Judge Harper. "Gentlemen, this is a situation where we're going to continue to get into trouble," the judge said. "The court overrules all motions and is denying your attempt to stop the trial."[6]

Foreman next attempted to re-submit six pre-trial motions that Harper had previously ruled against. Harper ruled the same way again. He also rejected two new requests to suppress the jury panel and to give the defense copies of testimony by government witnesses.

Testimony began Wednesday morning. Quickly on and off the stand were Martha Rahn, St. Louis court reporter who transcribed the proceedings of the federal grand jury in April, 1964, and Donald A. Hansen, Justice Department attorney who questioned Cargill during the grand jury.

Hugh A. Carroll, whose $40 million Selected Investments empire collapsed in 1957, pulling down three members of the Oklahoma Supreme Court in its wreckage, was called as the government's first major witness.

Carroll, a smallish, balding man of 79, told the jury that attorney O. A. Cargill masterminded the now-infamous Pierre Laval to explain away the $150,000 that he used to bribe former justice N. S. Corn. He said that when he related the fiction about Laval, he was acting on the advice of Cargill, who told him it was the "only way out," since the auditors were attempting to trace the $150,000 missing from the corporation. He said that Cargill recommended the Pierre Laval story rather than take the Fifth Amendment to explain the missing money.

Speaking easily and leaning back in his witness chair, Carroll told how he informed Cargill about the bribe at Cargill's home the day before the bankruptcy hearing for Selected Investments. He admitted that the plan to bribe Corn was "entirely my own," but said it was Cargill who suggested "we make up a story covering up the ($150,000) transaction. He outlined in general how the story could be told and suggested that it could be done because he had done so once or twice before."[7]

Carroll told the court, "I knew that something would come in regard to the $150,000 transaction. I had made up my mind to take the Fifth Amendment. I told him of the $150,000 I had delivered to Corn."

"What did Cargill say?" the prosecutor asked.

"He said he wished he had known about it--he could have handled it for less," Carroll answered, provoking a titter of laughter among the spectators. Judge Harper threatened to clear the courtroom if the demonstration was repeated.

At one point, Miskovsky produced a 1964 Montreal telephone

directory and waited while Carroll found a "Pierre Laval" listed in it.

Carroll said that following the bankruptcy hearing on March 17, 1958, where he testified to the loan to Laval, he and Cargill walked together from the federal building. "He (Cargill) told me he overheard the SEC (Securities and Exchange Commission) boys remark that that story showed that I, speaking of myself, was a smart SOB," Carroll said.[8]

U.S. Attorney Potter's questioning of Carroll was punctuated with frequent clashes by defense attorney Foreman, with Judge Harper sending the jury out several times to settle objections voiced by Foreman. He overruled most defense requests, but did sustain a motion to delete portions of Cargill's grand jury testimony not involved in the perjury indictment.

Cross-examination of Carroll was conducted by George Miskovsky, assistant counsel for the defense. Miskovsky repeatedly asked Carroll exact dates when certain things happened, and Carroll repeatedly said, "I don't recall that, George," or "After seven or eight years I wouldn't remember that, George." The two men had known each other for many years.[9]

Throughout it all, Cargill, wearing a light gray summer suit, sat impassively with his legs extended. Occasionally, he would cup his ear in order to hear better.

Under Miskovsky's questioning, Carroll admitted that he had been granted immunity from the county prosecutor and that he had received a full presidential pardon from President Lyndon Johnson. Miskovsky asked Carroll whether the pardon extended to the "perjury you committed," a reference to Carroll's testimony in federal bankruptcy court that he had given the $150,000 to Laval.

"It is full and complete," Carroll replied.

"You have been granted immunity by the county and by the federal prosecutor?" Miskovsky asked.

Carroll nodded.

Asked if the presidential pardon was the prosecutor's idea, Carroll said he did it on his own. He told the jury that he and his wife had been in Hartford, Connecticut, late in October and went from there to Washington. "We stopped at the Justice Department," he related. "They gave us the blanks and told us what to do."[10]

Carroll had received a five-year sentence for mail fraud after the Selected Investments bankruptcy and served 20 months in federal prison at Seagoville, Texas.

Jurors fidgeted in their chairs as the meticulous cross-examination continued on into Thursday morning. As testimony became more detailed and less spectacular, the crowd of spectators which had been overflowing the room earlier was now thinned to about half. On numerous occasions, some members of the jury could be seen watching the spectators rather than the witness.

Throughout it all, the defense attorneys remained quiet except for an occasional objection voiced by David Kline.

On and off the stand very quickly was Paul Copeland, local manager for Brinks, Inc. He testified as to the delivery of $150,000 in $100 bills in April, 1957 from First National Bank to Hugh Carroll at his downtown office.

Next on the witness stand was Mrs. Hugh Carroll, who told of meeting Cargill in early March, 1958, a day or two before the Selected bankruptcy hearing. Cargill had represented Selected three times previously, she said, in the state court receivership, at a hearing before the state securities commission, and in the early part of the bankruptcy case.

She told of going with her husband to Cargill's home, and she said, "I told Mr. Cargill that I didn't approve or like the idea of the Pierre Laval story he had suggested my husband tell to cover the $150,000 payment.

"He told me I didn't have any choice but to go along with the story, that there wasn't any other way," Mrs. Carroll added. "He spoke in a loud voice and used many oaths which I did not appreciate."[11]

Under cross-examination, it was brought out that Mrs. Carroll was a stenographer and rose to be corporate secretary of Selected Investments over a period of 20 years and married Carroll in 1952.

Former Justice N. S. Corn waited outside the courtroom all afternoon Thursday, ready to testify in the third day of the perjury trial of O. A. Cargill, Sr. However, extensive cross-examination of Hugh Carroll and questioning of Carroll's wife delayed Corn's appearance.

When he finally did reach the stand on Friday morning, the 81-year-old justice told a story that stunned the courtroom observers into silence. For citizens who thought they had heard the last of the supreme court scandal, his words ricocheted around the capitol like a high-powered bullet.

Almost nonchalantly, Corn answered the questions of U.S. Attorney Potter with the ease of a person recounting the names of his own children. The story that unfolded was a sordid tale of various alleged supreme court fixes. Corn, who had served on the Oklahoma Supreme Court for 24 years from 1935 to 1959, was asked, "Did you ever have any financial transactions with the defendant, O. A. Cargill?"

"Yes, I did," Corn replied.

"When was the first one?" Potter asked.

"Nineteen hundred and thirty six."

"Where?"

"In Mr. Cargill's office in the Hales Building (107 N. Robinson)."

Potter then asked Corn to describe the circumstances.

Corn said, "He called me to his office. He said he and several other lawyers had been discussing me and the kind of a judge they thought I made.

"He said he liked to be friendly with all the judges and he hoped that I would be friendly enough to be the sixth man in cases in which he was interested. I told him on a nine-member court, five was a majority and I didn't think I'd be much good as the sixth man.

"He said he didn't like to win by a bare majority. He said I was the kind of man he would like to keep on the court and he would furnish all the money I would need in campaigns. I told him $1,000 was all the law allowed me to spend.

"He said the first thing he wanted was to build me up a campaign fund. I told him there were 12 counties in my district and over 400 voting precincts. He thought it would be a good idea for me to go out on weekends and keep up my contacts in the counties. If I got to one each month, that would give me an opportunity to be in each once during a year."

Corn said he agreed to go along and that this was the way in which it took place. He said Cargill "would call me over the telephone, give me the number and style of the case. He'd say follow the majority or follow the crowd. Each time Cargill called him up, Corn said he would make a note on a piece of paper and put it in his desk. When the case was disposed of, he would then destroy the piece of paper.

He said he had dealings with Cargill with regard to three cases beginning in 1955. They were *Marshall v. Amos, Selected Investments Corp. v. The Oklahoma Tax Commission,* and *The Oklahoma Company v. O'Neil.*

The ex-justice then electrified the courtroom and sent reporters scurrying for the telephones with his next revelation. He told the court that very soon after the appeal was filed in *Marshall v. Amos* in 1955, Cargill "called me on the telephone and said, 'get your pencil and paper, I want to give you a case.' He said he had a big deal for $25,000 to be divided six ways, with $4,500 for me."

"What did you tell him, Judge?" Potter asked.

"I told him I would."

"I asked him who else was on the opinion." He said "The two Indians, Davison, Halley and Blackbird." (Corn identified the "two Indians" as Earl Welch and N. B. Johnson.)

"He said all five would go along?" Potter asked.

Corn replied that Cargill told him, "I have an attorney at Tulsa to take care of Halley and an attorney in Bristow to take care of

Blackbird, and I'm going to take care of Davison and the two Indians."[12]

Corn landed a bombshell. The courtroom fell silent. In barely five seconds, and with no forewarning, a cloud was thrown over the chief justice of the supreme court, Harry L. S. Halley, the immediate past chief justice, W. H. Blackbird, and veteran member Denver Davison. Until this moment, none of the three had been linked to bribery allegations. And this was the rankest kind of hearsay.

Reached at the capitol, an angry Justice Davison said, "Nobody ever paid me a bribe. I concurred in the *Oklahoma Company* case, but I dissented all the way in the other case *(Marshall v. Amos)*."

Davison told newsmen, "This is terrible. It just makes me sick to think about it. I know," Davison continued, "that during the bar investigation Corn was asked about each member of the court, whether they had accepted bribes, and when they came to my name he said, 'Oh, no, no!'"

Justice Halley asserted, "I deny this flat-footed and unequivocally. I never heard of Cargill being in the case until long after it was decided." He said, "Nobody approached me about that or has ever said anything to me about the case."

Justice Blackbird was not at the capitol when reporters arrived. Reached later he said, "I just want to say that neither Mr. O. A. Cargill nor any other person approached me or would dare to approach me with a bribe. As to whether Mr. Cargill made this statement, I don't know.

"It is ridiculous," Blackbird continued, "and a shame that this court has to put up with such tomfoolery as we've had to put up with lately. We've had our names dragged through the press and TV to the point where it is sickening."[13]

U.S. Attorney Potter asked Corn if he ever received the $4,000 from Cargill.

"A few days later after the mandate came down, he (Cargill) called me and said he would be ready in a day or two." Corn related that Cargill called the next day to say that he had received a check but his name was on it and he didn't want to be involved for tax reasons. Cargill called again the following day and said everything was all right and he was ready to pay. Corn's recollection was that he received the money in $100 bills in front of the Hales Building in downtown Oklahoma City.

Corn told the jury that after Hugh Carroll had agreed to pay $150,000 for a favorable tax decision in the *Selected Investments* case, he called Cargill and told him about the deal and told him he would give him $2,500 if he would get Carlile to go along." (This was a reference to the late justice Lon Carlile.)

"He (Cargill) said Carlile would vote any way he wanted him to."

"Did you pay the defendant (Cargill)?" Potter asked.

"Yes, sir, I did," Corn replied. "I called him one evening about 3:30 or later. I told him I had the money. He said he had his hat on and was just leaving the building and would see me the next morning. He met me then, reached in the car, and got the money." Corn stated that "Welch, Johnson, Davison, Williams, Carlile and myself voted for the opinion and the other three dissented."[14]

Corn stated that in 1958 Cargill called him and said, "you had better have Carroll hire me (Cargill)." He said this should be done so that Cargill could take care of the Selected "situation." (This was a reference to the Selected bankruptcy hearing.) Corn said he called Carroll as suggested, and Cargill told him the next day that he received a call from Carroll within moments after their first conversation.

According to Corn, Cargill called sometime later and said, "I've got everything fixed. Carroll will testify tomorrow that he let a Canadian have the money in some kind of an oil transaction." He went on to quote Cargill as saying, "I'm having trouble with Mrs. Carroll."

The ex-justice said Cargill called him later and informed him, "'I've got Mrs. Carroll lined up. Everything is going to be all right'."

Asked by Potter about the *Oklahoma Company v. O'Neil* case which was decided in 1958, the ex-justice said, "Mr. Cargill called me on a Saturday morning. He wanted me to come to his place. I drove up on the east side and he came out and got in my car.

"He said there had been a case filed up here 'I've got to get reversed. It involves my daughter and son-in-law. I'll give you, Judge Welch and Judge Johnson $2,500 each to get that case reversed.'

"I told him I'd take it up with Welch and Johnson. He didn't have the number or the style of the case but said he would call me up."

Corn said he talked to Welch and Johnson individually. "I never did talk to them together," he said. "I told them Cargill wanted the case reversed. His daughter was involved. I thought we ought to help him if we could."

Welch, Johnson, Carlile, Davison and Corn voted to reverse the lower court. The other three justices voted to sustain it.

Corn continued, "Mr. Cargill called me several days later and said he was ready to pay off. I drove down to the Hales Building. He was waiting on the street. I took the money to my office and counted it out in three equal piles."[15]

Corn revealed that in late 1963, about five or six months before he was indicted for income tax evasion, he called Cargill and told him he thought John Speck was assisting the federal investigators in his case and that Cargill ought to stop Speck. Cargill wanted to know why. Corn said he told Cargill, "You ought to tell him you got $2,500 out of the $150,000 you told John Speck I received from Hugh Carroll.

"I told him (Cargill), 'I'm not going on the witness stand and swear one bit for you. What would you think if I told the government about the $4,000 in the *Marshall v. Amos* case, $2,500 in the *Selected Investments* case and the $2,500 in the *Oklahoma Company* case'?

"That seemed to make him mad," the ex-justice observed dryly. Cargill shouted at him, "When I get through with you, nobody in the world will believe what you say."[16]

Corn's initial testimony took just 35 minutes. He was on the stand another four hours, though, under intense cross-examination by chief defense counsel Foreman.

Asked by Foreman why he failed to vote for an opinion favorable to Cargill's clients on some cases, Corn implicated Cargill in "deals" with other attorneys as well.

Foreman cited, one at a time, a dozen supreme court cases in which Cargill's clients lost. "I suggest that you didn't vote in five, that you voted against him in four, and that you authored an opinion against him in yet another one," Foreman declared.

"He didn't call me on those cases, or he called me and told me that he had the same kind of deal with the other side, and I voted the way I wanted to," Corn replied.

Asked if he meant the attorneys on the other side, Corn replied, "That's right."

Questioned further, Corn added that it was "the same deal and that it didn't make any difference for me to vote however I wanted to."

Figuring the $4,500 in campaign funds received from Cargill into his years on the bench, Foreman asked him if it weren't true that he was "working for less than 30 cents a day for Mr. Cargill?"

"I never did do any figuring," Corn said.

"You were selling your oath of office for this pittance of money? Correct?"

Corn turned toward Judge Harper and said, "I don't believe he has worded that so I can give an intelligent answer, has he Judge?"

"That's up to you," Judge Harper replied.

Then Corn said, "I violated my oath and I ruined myself completely, disgraced my family, disappointed my friends. The only thing left for me to do now is come in and tell the truth, and that's what I'm doing."

Foreman asked Corn what he did with the $150,000 bribe paid

him by Hugh Carroll. Corn said he gave $7,500 each to Welch and Johnson.

"What did you do with the money after you got it?"

"I spent it in various ways."

Corn said he kept some in a pair of old shoes in a locker at Lincoln Park golf course, buried some in fruit jars in his yard, and had other bills in filing cabinets at his capitol office and at home. When Carroll told him in March, 1958, that he needed the money back, Corn gave him $33,000. But that wasn't all he had, he told the jury.

"I told him I'd turn back all that was available," Corn said, adding, "I could have got some more, I guess" from other hiding places.

Corn said the money was all gone after he paid taxes with interest and penalties and bought a new car.[17]

The trial recessed for the weekend. The jury remained sequestered under guard at the Skirvin Hotel in downtown Oklahoma City.

When court resumed on Monday, June 7, defense attorney Foreman resumed his methodical questioning of ex-justice N. S. Corn, focusing on his gambling activities in an attempt to trace the $150,000 he received as a bribe. Corn told of gambling trips to race tracks in Hot Springs, Arkansas; Omaha, Nebraska; Chicago, Illinois; and New Mexico. He also told of a week-long trip in 1957 to Las Vegas gaming tables.

Under continued questioning by Foreman, Corn admitted that he played poker with former governors Leon C. "Red" Phillips and Roy Turner. He also admitted he played "friendly poker" with Robert S. Kerr, who later became governor and U.S. Senator.

Late Monday morning, Corn stated that he had no personal knowledge of bribes being given to the three justices, Halley, Blackbird, and Davison.

Foreman asked specifically about Davison, but Corn's answer referred to his testimony Friday, which named all three.

"I do not have personal knowledge...I was just making a

statement of what Cargill told me,'' Corn said.

He added, ''They tried to bring it out before the senate (impeachment), but (Justice N. B.) Johnson was the defendant there, and they told me it would be hearsay.''[18]

On Saturday, the state bar association had issued a statement defending the three justices, whom it had cleared of bribery implications a month before. The committee criticized the news media for an ''erroneous interpretation'' of Corn's testimony.

''Corn had not himself implicated the three judges; he did quote Cargill as implicating the judges,'' the statement said.

The statement further noted, ''It seems not inappropriate to note that Cargill is not on trial for telling the truth.''

The bar urged the public to ''wait until the evidence is in.''

Corn was back on the witness stand for a third day of testimony when court opened on Tuesday morning. Defense counsel Foreman dropped all pretense of politeness and hammered away at Corn's possible motives for implicating Cargill.

''Have you ever accused O. A. Cargill of attempting to extort $20,000 by way of a fee out of you to represent you in the tax case?'' Foreman demanded.

''Well, I put it in my statement up at Springfield,'' Corn replied, a reference to the 84-page sworn statement he gave state and federal attorneys before he was released from the federal prison hospital at Springfield, Missouri.

''Is there any person in the world you hate more sincerely than O. A. Cargill?''

''Well, I try not to hate anybody, but it's hard for me to like any man who did what O. A. Cargill did to me,'' Corn answered.

Foreman repeated the question.

Corn replied, ''I don't think there's a man in the world I dislike more than O. A. Cargill. I don't recall anyone at this time.''

His response prompted Cargill to cover his face momentarily and silently move his lips.

Corn testified that he went to Cargill's office on February 6,

1961, to employ him to represent Corn against the tax evasion charges. Further testimony revealed that he fired Cargill two weeks later.

Foreman asked Corn if he had seen Cargill in the Oklahoma City federal building in September, 1963. Corn said the only time he had seen Cargill was in March, 1962.

"Did you say, 'I will ruin you for turning me in to the Internal Revenue Service'" Foreman asked.

"I never did make that statement in my life." Corn repeated the denial several times in response to persistent questioning by Foreman.

"The only statement I made to O. A. Cargill in the federal building was in March (1962).... I shook hands with him and looked him in the eye and told him, 'You didn't handle my case the way you would have handled yours or Buck's.' Buck's his son, you know."[19]

At 11:57 a.m., Corn's cross-examination was ended. He had testified for two-and-a-half days. Corn had spoken thousands of words during that time, but perhaps none carried as many implications as those he spoke on Monday: "Now, the story's never been half told, with everything that took place."

Signs of impending trouble on the defense team flared up right after the court recessed for lunch. Percy Foreman and George Miskovsky were heard to exchange heated words in the presence of a reporter in the nearly deserted courtroom.

Foreman accused Miskovsky with interrupting and/or interfering with his procedures in the case. Miskovsky was heard to deny the accusation, saying, "That's a lie."

Foreman also criticized Miskovsky for "wearing your feelings on your sleeve."

"I am not," replied Miskovsky, who then turned and walked out with his arm draped over the shoulder of Cargill.[20]

Following Corn to the stand was H. G. Marshall, a former Oklahoma City drilling contractor who was a principal in the

Marshall v. Amos case in 1956. He testified that Cargill told him he had "a dangerous lawsuit" and that Marshall should hire Cargill to defend him. "He said I stood a chance of losing it and that it would take $30,000 to win the lawsuit from the boys on the hill," said Marshall.

The case involved a Cleveland County oil lease that contained eight wells. Marshall said he had lost the 1953 district court lawsuit and appealed it to the supreme court in 1955. The court reversed the decision in 1965.

Marshall told the jury that he arranged the $30,000 payment to Cargill with the stipulation that the case must be reversed and the mandate furnished Marshall before paying Cargill. The witness said he got the cashier's check drawn off the First National Bank of Wichita Falls, Texas, after Cargill declined to accept payment in cash. Marshall said the payment was made in Cargill's office.

A receipt from Cargill for the money was introduced by Assistant U.S. Attorney David Kline, noting that it was a receipt to Ida B. Marshall for legal services in the case of Amos against Marshall et al.

"Did Cargill make any appearance before the supreme court (in that appeal)?" Kline asked.

"Well, uh, no," Marshall replied.

"Did he write any briefs?"

"No, sir," Marshall answered.

Marshall also said he had been subpoenaed last fall to appear at the trial of Earl Welch in Muskogee, where the former justice was convicted of income tax evasion.

"I called Cargill up and told him two boys out of Washington had talked to me and I showed them all the records I had." Cargill wanted to know how he came out.

"He told me I'd better keep my damned mouth shut, if you know what I mean." Marshall did not testify at the trial.[21]

On cross-examination, Percy Foreman's questions centered on Cargill's prior work for Marshall. Foreman seemed intent on proving that the $30,000 was payment for past legal services rendered by Cargill covering the past 37 years.

Marshall testified that "Cargill handled a few small cases for me and one large one."

Foreman dwelt at length on the fact that Marshall had never paid Cargill for his legal services covering 37 years.

"I don't think I owed him anything...and he never asked me for anything or sent me an invoice," Marshall responded.

Asked directly by Foreman, "Did Cargill ever indicate to you that he had connections with the Supreme Court of Oklahoma?" Marshall emphatically replied, "Yes, sir."

Foreman noted that Marshall had told just the opposite to the bar committee in an October 29 interview.

Marshall said, "I knew what he could do and the influence he had. I figured it was good insurance to pay him $30,000 to keep somebody from approaching him, and him maybe getting on the other side of the fence."

Marshall and Foreman repeatedly interrupted each other during cross-examination. Marshall was intent on volunteering "all I know that's the truth," while Foreman became irked that the witness kept explaining the case instead of answering specific questions.[22]

Finally, Judge Harper admonished both men for arguing with each other.

Wednesday's session opened with Foreman still questioning Marshall in relation to the *Marshall v. Amos* case. A legal hassle developed as Foreman attempted to introduce records of a series of arrests of Marshall on bogus check charges.

Judge Harper ordered the jury from the room while defense and prosecution attorneys argued whether the arrests and the one conviction were admissible as evidence to impeach Marshall's credibility. Harper ruled the information inadmissible for the time being, but ordered each side to prepare arguments showing what the Oklahoma law provides about entering such evidence.

Wednesday afternoon, Foreman read from what was purported to be a series of questions asked Marshall at his home by two teams of private investigators hired by Cargill. Marshall emphatically and repeatedly denied making the statements, many of them hostile towards Cargill.

Thursday was the eighth day of the trial and H. G. Marshall was still on the stand. His appearance was delayed, however, while the court took the testimony of Ardmore banker Felix Simmons, who for many years had been executive officer of Liberty National Bank of Oklahoma City. Recovering from major surgery, Simmons was flown up from Ardmore on a chartered plane by the defense. In deference to his ill health, he was put on the stand immediately.

Originally, Simmons had been listed as a witness for the prosecution to testify as to Corn allegedly paying off a mortgage, but because of his surgery they had excused him. Foreman then subpoenaed Simmons to appear, claiming that he would be the "star witness" who would "utterly discredit" the testimony of principal witness Justice N. S. Corn.

Simmons answered fewer than 50 questions in a firm and steady voice.

"Tell us whether, after (Liberty National Bank) moved from its former location on March 17, 1962, whether you had any transactions, money changing, with Mr. Corn," Foreman asked.

"Not as frequently as when we were at our former location (at Main and Robinson)." Simmons then testified that he had changed "various sizes" of large bills for Corn between 1947 and 1952.

"Were there any $1,000 bills?" Foreman asked.

"There might have been one or two," Simmons said.

"Were there any $500 bills?"

"Likewise--several."

The banker said it was difficult for him to remember how frequently Corn made the transactions because "we were in a gray-market area during that time, and a lot of money changed hands under the table...that money was brought into the bank and broken down from big bills." Simmons said his transactions with

Corn might have occurred as much as three or four times a month.

Corn had previously denied frequent transactions and testified to only three occasions when he used $500 bills. Corn said he paid off his home mortgage in 1936 with a $1,000 bill and a $500 bill from the first $1,500 "campaign" payment he received from O. A. Cargill.

Simmons said Corn might have, but that he did not specifically remember it.

In the eyes of most observers, the defense failed to score many points from its so-called star witness.

Marshall returned to the stand, and cross-examination resumed.

The defense scored a minor victory when it got Marshall to admit that the substance of the statements by private investigators was what he said to them. Marshall's reversal came after defense lawyers promised to call some of the investigators as witness and to offer tape recordings to back up their story.

The government's next-to-last witness was Titus Haffa, a Chicago industrialist who had guaranteed the $30,000 payment to Cargill.

Haffa was not far into his testimony, however, when the jury was ordered out of the courtroom and a blistering exchange erupted between Judge Harper and defense attorney Foreman.

Haffa had testified to a series of letters between Cargill and himself in 1956 in connection with the *Marshall v. Amos* case before the supreme court. He said that one letter was personally brought to him by H. G. Marshall for signature.

"Are you aware what perjury is?" Judge Harper asked, pointing his finger at him.

"I am," Haffa replied, seemingly startled.

"Then there is no need for me to explain it," Harper said. "Are you aware you testified earlier that that letter was mailed to you by Speers (identified as an attorney for Haffa)?"

Haffa said the judge was right and that he, Haffa, was confused.

With the jury out of the courtroom, Percy Foreman criticized the judge for ''undue fervor'' and unintentional ''intimidation'' of the witness.

''I've been on this court a long time and I have never allowed what appeared to be perjured testimony without calling it to the attention of the jury,'' Judge Harper told Foreman of Haffa's testimony. ''Obviously, this man is either mistaken or lying, and I intend to call it to his attention so he can tell the jury.''

Foreman objected to the judge's interruption, and said it should be done at the end of the testimony.

''I don't see why I should wait until it is over, because by then it could unduly influence the result,'' the judge explained.

Foreman emphasized that he was not questioning Judge Harper's motives, but said the judge's admonition was tending to ''so intimidate this witness as to interfere with cross-examination.''

Both men's voices rose to a near shout as the argument progressed.

''I know you wouldn't agree as to the time of day!'' Judge Harper snapped at one point.

Foreman asked the court to ''note my exception'' to Judge Harper's ruling.[23]

The government rested its case with the brief testimony of John E. Luttrell, Norman attorney and supreme court justice from 1947 until 1951. Luttrell said he alone represented H. G. Marshall in the Cleveland County oil lease case against H. D. Amos, Dallas, and in the supreme court appeal of that case.

Luttrell's testimony set the stage to refute Cargill's claim that the $30,000 paid by Marshall was for legal services.

12

Humbling the Haughty

The spotlight turned on O. A. Cargill, Sr., almost the forgotten man in the larger issues involved in his case. A striking figure, 6 feet 4 inches, broad shoulders, still a lion of a man at age 80, he stood erect as he walked through the corridors of the federal building.

The defense began its case with motions for a mistrial and for a directed verdict of acquittal. Assistant defense counsel Jack G. Day argued that the government failed to meet the minimum standards which require, in order to obtain a bribery conviction, that the government must obtain testimony of two independent witnesses. Day argued that "Corn, the principal witness, is certainly not independent."

He argued that the only corroboration for the Corn testimony came from H. G. Marshall that he paid $30,000 to Cargill to win a favorable decision from "the boys on the hill." At the very least, he said, Marshall's testimony is "ambiguous," and "it does not have the quality of certainty desired by the law."

Judge Harper overruled the defense motions without waiting for any argument from the government. He said the testimony showed Marshall had paid money to Cargill and Corn had received some of it.[1]

Chief defense attorney Percy Foreman began his opening statement. He recounted the personal history of the defendant, O. A. Cargill, Sr.: born in Arkansas; came to Indian Territory in

1901; deputy U.S. marshal from 1903 until 1907; elected constable of his district in the first election after statehood; served two terms as justice of the peace; worked as a streetcar motorman, conductor, and later as a policeman while obtaining a legal education; elected county attorney in 1923; soon after was elected mayor; member of the Oklahoma delegation to three Democratic National Conventions; listed in Who's Who for 25 years; author of several religious books; and received an honorary doctor's degree from Southern Baptist University at Walnut Ridge, Arkansas.[2]

He said that Cargill had studied theology at the Moody Bible Institute in Chicago. He had four children, 10 grandchildren, and 17 great-grandchildren, all living in Oklahoma. His sole asset was a piece of land north of Oklahoma City purchased at depression prices on which oil was found and was now worth $1 million.

The first defense witness was Merle Zweifel, a former inmate of the federal correctional institution at Seagoville, Texas, at the same time that Hugh Carroll, former head of Selected Investments Corp., was a prisoner there. Zweifel, age 53, said he lived in the same cottage as Carroll.

Speaking politely and in a quiet voice, Zweifel related a bizarre tale of $150,000 being buried under water. He said in August, 1959, Carroll told him that he had taken the $150,000 to Canada where he had a summer cottage. He said Carroll had "taken it to a place where he'd swum, been swimming, off a diving board or walkway about 20 paces."[3]

Court adjourned for the day before the government could conduct its cross-examination and Zweifel was ordered to return the following morning.

Defense counsel Foreman informed the court that he was unable to estimate the number of witnesses he would call, but he said he would include "reputable citizens" of Oklahoma City and most members of the supreme court.

He further stated that contrary to earlier indications, he would not call former Justices N. B. Johnson and Earl Welch. Foreman said it would be "professionally improper" to call either gentleman since they were in litigation which might relate to the Cargill case.[4]

At the outset of Friday's session, the defense filed a motion for a continuance or a mistrial because of an illness that would prevent M. A. (Ned) Looney, prominent Oklahoma City attorney, from testifying.

Judge Harper rebuked the defense as he denied the motion. He pointed out that the day the trial started, June 1, the defense sought a continuance because of Looney's illness, when it had known for weeks before that Looney could not appear.

The judge said Looney is "in such a condition this court feels the defendant should have been in a position to making a showing at the time the case was called for trial." He pointed out that all the defense did was ask for permission to file an oral motion.

At the same time, Judge Harper said the defense also asked for a continuation based on the belief that Johnson was too ill to appear. "Then," said Harper, referring to Foreman's statement to the jury Thursday afternoon, "you got up and told the jury you were not going to use him, and made a speech.

"You subpoenaed Welch and had him there on the opening day of the trial. Yesterday you announced you wouldn't call him, and I had asked him to be available at a phone call."[5]

Called back to the stand on Friday morning, Merle Zweifel, under cross-examination by Assistant U.S. Attorney David A. Kline, had gaping holes punched in his credibility. He admitted two convictions for mail fraud, one in 1948 and one in 1957, and also making a plea of guilty in Latimer County, Oklahoma, to the unlawful sale of land.

"Did you not know that on December 9, 1959, Mr. Carroll's state court conviction was reversed?" asked Kline.

"No, I didn't know that."

"He didn't tell you?"

"No, sir."

"Didn't you know his attorneys visited him several times?"

"No, sir."

The entire supreme court was called to testify in Cargill's behalf. In fact, we were issued subpoenas which required our attendance. The only one they didn't subpoena was Ralph Hodges, the newest justice, who was appointed only two months earlier to replace Earl Welch. The ninth place on the bench was still vacant, following the impeachment of N. B. Johnson.

Chief Justice Harry L. S. Halley was in Louisiana for a troop review. Percy Foreman said he would call him later.

Justice Denver Davison was called first. "Tell us, please," Foreman asked of Davison, "whether O. A. Cargill, Sr., ever paid, offered to pay or promised to pay any money to you or if he has ever promised to give you anything of value?"

"No, sir," replied Davison, "he never gave me anything."

"Have you at any time since you have been on the court had any financial transactions with O. A. Cargill, Sr.?"

"No, sir."

"Did you vote to concur in *Oklahoma v. O'Neil?*"

"Yes."

In cross-examination, Kline asked Davison if he had any knowledge of any telephone conversation between Cargill and Corn about a court payoff.

"None whatsoever," Davison replied.

Justice Williams, when he was asked whether Cargill had given him anything of value, paused for a moment. "He hasn't as far as I know. He hasn't paid me any money."

In response to the question regarding financial transactions with Cargill, Williams answered, "I have not."

Similarly, Justice Blackbird answered the questions, "No, sir" and "I have not."

When it came my turn to testify, I stated that I had never had any financial dealings with Cargill. Also, I pointed out I did not go on the supreme court until after Corn had retired, and I had received nothing from Cargill since becoming a member.[6]

Mrs. O. A. Cargill followed the supreme court justices to the witness stand.

Speaking in a small but clear voice, Mrs. Cargill recalled that Mr. and Mrs. Hugh Carroll had been at their house on a Saturday afternoon before the Selected Investments bankruptcy hearing and had spent about an hour. When reminded that Carroll previously testified that it was during this visit that Cargill had given him the general outline of the Pierre Laval story, Mrs. Cargill said she was with Mrs. Carroll during the entire visit.

"At any time, did O. A. Cargill mention the name Pierre Laval?" Foreman asked.

"No sir," she said.

Asked if she noticed "any unusual conversation between your husband and Mrs. Julia Carroll," Mrs. Cargill repeated, "No, sir."

"Was there any discussion whatever about any testimony about anything?" Foreman asked.

"No, sir," she replied.

Asked if anything about any testimony was said during a ride to see the buffalo on Cargill's ranch, Mrs. Cargill repeated her earlier negative answer.

"Have Hugh Carroll and Julia Carroll ever been to your house except on this one occasion?" Foreman asked.

"No, sir," was her final reply.[7]

Five Oklahoma City attorneys took the stand in rapid succession. Each had opposed Cargill on supreme court cases and had won. Taking the stand were attorneys Duke Duval, Mart Brown, T. Murray Robinson, Clayton B. Pierce and Kenneth J. Wilson.

After asking each about the specific lawsuit which he had won in the high court, Foreman asked:

"Did you have any arrangement, understanding or agreement with O. A. Cargill or his firm in the lawsuit which they lost and you won whereby Cargill or the Cargill firm would profit by losing the case?''

Their answers were all negative.[8]

Kline then asked each whether he had personal knowledge of the ''conversations, conduct, or facts'' material to the perjury trial. Each answered, ''No.''

Three character witnesses appeared on Friday. They were Edgar T. Bell, general manager of KWTV; C. A. Vose, board chairman of First National Bank; and I. L. Yearby, long-time Baptist minister.[9]

The strains that were evident in the defense team on Wednesday reached a head on Friday. When the court reassembled after the noon recess, Miskovsky requested permission from trial Judge Roy Harper to be absent in open court for the rest of the trial.

''Mr. Cargill employed me to perform certain professional services. But those services were finished at the close of the prosecutor's testimony,'' he told Harper.

Although Miskovsky and Foreman had a friendly courtroom departure, Miskovsky earlier admitted that he and Foreman had ''differences of opinion'' on trial matters. Asked about Wednesday's scene, Miskovsky sought to minimize the differences. He said it was just a minor quarrel and that Foreman was trying to point out that he preferred having notes handed to him instead of being interrupted during cross-examination of government witnesses.

Miskovsky said he had previously arranged to leave this weekend on a 40-day world tour with his family and some 30 members of the University of Oklahoma Alumni Association.

Confusion reigned Saturday morning as defense attorney Foreman and Cargill's accountant consistently misunderstood each other.

The morning began all right with a series of character witnesses, including former Governor W. J. Holloway. Other witnesses included the Rev. Bill C. Haggard of Highland Hills Baptist Church; Elmer Harber, Shawnee banker; and Mrs. Phyllis Burbage, a former employee of the Cargill firm.

But things deteriorated rapidly when Foreman called accountant Joseph H. Hill to the stand, with records. Foreman tried to explore the various bank accounts held by Cargill and his firm during the past 20 years. When it became clear that Foreman and the accountant were confused, Judge Harper called a brief recess for the two to confer.

When Hill resumed testifying, Foreman asked the accountant to detail all checks issued by Cargill or his firm in October, November and December, 1958, and January, 1959. However, Hill was apparently still confused, for he noted a half dozen checks before Foreman realized that the accountant was in the 1956 accounts. Among the checks inadvertently revealed were one to Wayne Bayless for $15,000, dated October 24, 1956, and labeled "refund legal services, Ida Marshall," and a $7,500 check to Cargill's son with the same date and notation. (Bayless, an attorney at the time, was a former supreme court justice.)

Assistant U.S. Attorney Kline objected to the records search, saying that the government had never contended that an alleged payment to former Justice Corn was made by check, but that it was made in cash.

Judge Harper interrupted Hill at one point to clarify what year's checks were being discussed and which of the several checking accounts.

Kline again tried to speed up the morning session. "If Mr. Foreman would just tell us what he is trying to prove, it's entirely possible the government would agree," he said.

Foreman refused, but at another point he put his hand to his forehead and stammered:

"Are we--Oh, Lord, now I'm mixed up."[10]

The 80-year-old O. A. Cargill, Sr., took the witness stand in his own behalf Saturday afternoon. In three hours of testimony, he repeatedly denied he had ever given money to any supreme court justice to influence decisions.

At first, he nervously fingered an index card, turning it over and over in his hands, rubbing it against his face. At one point, he remarked, "I'm a little bit nervous." His nervousness gradually disappeared as the interrogation by Percy Foreman continued.

"Tell us whether or not you have a successful law practice?" Foreman asked.

"I did have...until this (the indictment) came up," Cargill replied.

Then Cargill contradicted testimony given earlier by former Justice Corn. He denied he ever had any financial transactions with Corn except possibly some small campaign contributions, or that he had ever agreed to underwrite any campaign or travel expenses for Corn.

"Did you ever receive $2,500 from Corn for the purpose of giving it to a judge now dead named W. A. Carlile?" Foreman asked.

"I never did," Cargill replied, adding, "Carlile was a good man."

"Other than campaign expenses, have you ever had any financial transactions with any supreme court judges of the state of Oklahoma?" Foreman asked.

"I have not," Cargill answered.

Foreman then asked Cargill a series of questions pertaining to Hugh Carroll and the $150,000 purportedly paid to the fictional Pierre Laval.

Cargill denied any knowledge of the story or how it was created, other than the fact that he was present at the hearing in which Carroll told the story. Cargill also denied that Hugh Carroll had ever told him about paying $150,000 to Justice Corn.

In response to the prior testimony of H. G. Marshall that the $30,000 cashier's check was to "pay the boys on the hill," Cargill said that the $30,000 payment was for past legal services. He said he had done work for Marshall prior to that case in 1954-56 and had never been paid for it. "Our agreement, at my suggestion that I would like to be protected in my fee, was if, as and when they won the lawsuit in *Marshall v. Amos,* Marshall would pay all due from the Noble County suit."

"Did you ever state to Marshall or anyone else that any part of that ($30,000) was to go to any judges of the supreme court?" Foreman asked.

"I did not," Cargill replied, adding that he had "no connection" with the case at all and hadn't discussed it with any judges when it was pending before the supreme court.

Percy Foreman and Judge Harper clashed again when Foreman was asking Cargill a series of detailed questions about the *Meadors* case.

"Mr. Foreman," Harper interrupted, "what in the world does that have with this lawsuit?"

Foreman attempted to explain that he was trying to show that apparently half of the $30,000 fee from Marshall went to Wayne Bayless for the *Meadors* case.[11]

Before Cargill returned to the stand again on Wednesday morning, Chief Justice Halley was called to testify that at no time did he ever receive anything of value from Cargill or have any financial transactions with Cargill. His testimony was the same as the other members of the supreme court who were called as witnesses on Friday.

Kline began his cross-examination of Cargill by referring to testimony he had given Saturday that he did not drink, smoke or use profane language. Kline then asked Cargill to explain an incident on November 4, 1952, and asked if it was not true that he had used profane and bellicose language on that day.

After an outburst of argument from the defense, Cargill's answer was, "Yes." He said he was stopped by three policemen, whom he did not know, for running a red light. He said they told him they were going to impound his car and take him down to the station, and the discussion grew "very heated."

There was no further reference to the incident and Kline turned to other subjects.

Kline was unable to shake Cargill's earlier testimony that the $15,000 check to Bayless was for payment in connection with the *Meadors* case, despite the fact that the canceled check bore the notation, "Refund Ida Marshall." Kline brought out that the will case was finally decided in December, 1955, and that Cargill did not pay Bayless until October, 1956, when he got the $30,000 from Marshall.

Asked about the delay, Cargill replied, "Bayless would have waited two years for me to pay him. He knew I was good for it."[12]

Kline asked Cargill about any conversations he may have had with Purcell publisher James C. Nance and Mrs. Laura A. Fleming. "Did you not go to Purcell on a Sunday while the *Meadors* case was pending before the supreme court and talk to Mr. Nance, and, in effect, offer him $10,000 if he would talk to Justice Floyd L. Jackson?"

Cargill said he spoke at the First Baptist Church in Purcell and recalled talking to Nance, but said he did not remember whether the will case was discussed.

"After you made the proposition, didn't Mr. Nance say, in effect, 'Jackson couldn't be touched with a 100-foot pole'?"

"He might have said that if I inquired about him (Jackson)," Cargill replied.

Kline then asked if Cargill told Nance that Cargill "owned the supreme court, or words to that effect."

Cargill denied making such a statement to anyone, including Nance and Mrs. Fleming.[13]

The defense ended its case at noon.

The government called the first of its two rebuttal witnesses, Mrs. Laura A. Fleming, to the stand. Mrs. Fleming repeated almost word for word a portion of the affidavit she filed in 1948 in connection with a case she had before the supreme court. The affidavit came to light during the impeachment trial of former Justice N. B. Johnson.

Under questioning by U.S. Attorney B. Andrew Potter, she said that Cargill had told her:

"You see how you lost your case in the lower court. Well, you'll lose a damn sight worse in the supreme court because I have a majority of those folks fixed out there, too, from Chief Justice Corn on down and there are nine judges out there.

"You better think this over, folks, while I'm still in the notion to give you $1,200 for your lease and possibly $500 for your travel expenses."

James C. Nance, publisher and former legislator, was the second and last rebuttal witness. He testified that Cargill offered him $10,000 to use his friendship with Justice Floyd Jackson in order to influence his vote in the 1955 *Meadors* case.

The 71-year-old publisher's testimony was the government's final attempt at tightening the noose around O. A. Cargill, Sr. He testified that Cargill met with him in his newspaper office and explained that the high court was divided four and four on the *Meadors* case and that Jackson held the deciding vote.

"He wanted to know if I could influence Justice Jackson and said if I could he would want to pay me a good fee. I recall it was $10,000.

"I said to Mr. Cargill that I knew Justice Jackson pretty well and that if there is an honest man on the court it is Justice Jackson," said Nance.

Under cross-examination, Nance said he didn't know any details of the case, including the $1,250,000 the attorneys stood to win in the lawsuit.

Defense attorney Foreman also tried to show that Nance was a close friend of Ned Looney, one of the lawyers opposing Cargill in the case. The publisher said Looney's name had never come up in the conversation.[14]

Cargill took the stand briefly to rebut Nance's testimony. He said he never phoned Nance, but that he was in Purcell that particular Sunday at the Baptist church there, and that he accidentally ran into Nance on the street. He said the two started discussing the Meadors case and mentioned that Jackson was a new man on the court.

Cargill said he asked if Jackson, being a friend of Looney's, might lean toward that side. "I don't think you can touch Jackson with a 100-foot pole," Cargill recalled Nance as saying.

The 80-year-old Cargill's voice cracked slightly under the strain.[15]

At 3:30 p.m. on Tuesday, the case went to the jury. Each side had been allocated two-and-a-half hours for closing arguments, followed by nearly an hour of instructions from Judge Harper.

Harper told the jurors they must return a separate verdict in all three counts. In his instructions, the judge read the entire grand jury indictment, emphasizing that they would have to find Cargill had willfully and knowingly committed the perjury.

"The issue is not whether he gave the testimony," Judge Harper said. He said the jury should decide whether the testimony alleged by Cargill and set out in the indictment was false, and was known to be false at the time he gave it, and that he intended to give the false testimony.

Harper asked the jurors to reach the verdict in a "calm, cool and deliberate manner," adding that their decision on each of the three counts had to be unanimous.

As the jurors filed out of the courtroom, O. A. "Buck" Cargill, Jr., left his seat in the spectators portion and took a chair next to his father at the defense table. David Cargill, grandson, had remained at Cargill's side throughout the trial.

The jury took a break for dinner at 6:20 p.m., and returned shortly after 8:00 p.m. About an hour later, they requested a special 45 minutes of testimony review.

At 1:07 a.m., Wednesday morning, after deliberating seven hours, the jurors filed back into the courtroom.

Jury foreman Hugh R. Hughes of Cushing, Oklahoma, delivered the verdict: Guilty on all three counts.

After the verdict was read, David Cargill covered his face with his hand. His grandfather gave him a reassuring pat on the back and the younger man straightened up in his chair.

Many relatives--several of them weeping and sobbing openly--crowded around Cargill as he slowly walked from the courtroom.

Faced by a woman reporter, Cargill said simply, ''Goodbye, sister,'' and walked on.

13

Rebuilding Justice

The past 14 months had been a sorry time for the image of justice in Oklahoma. In that brief span, three Oklahoma judges had been disgraced and two members of powerful legal families had been toppled from their niche. Of these, O. A. Cargill, Sr., was the last of the mighty oaks to fall.[1]

In summary, this fateful series of events began on April 8, 1964, when a federal grand jury returned indictments for income tax evasion against Supreme Court Justices N. S. Corn and Earl Welch. Since that date, Corn pled *nolo contendere* and served part of an 18-month sentence. Earl Welch was convicted and sentenced to three years, currently on appeal, and resigned from the high court in the face of impeachment proceedings. His brother, Lee Welch was also convicted of tax evasion, stemming from testimony given during the ex-justice's trial, and in April, 1965, was sentenced to 18 months in prison. Justice N. B. Johnson was impeached and removed from office on charges of corruption and bribery.

Yet, after all of this evidence of corruption, the Oklahoma legislature was no closer to judicial reform. Various reform proposals had been put forward to strengthen the bench and the bar, but there was little hope of any of them coming out of the legislature.

Governor Henry Bellmon sounded the tocsin bell. In a formal

statement issued following Johnson's impeachment, he said:

"All citizens have been witnessing the recent developments regarding the Oklahoma Supreme Court and now at the conclusion of the proceedings before the Oklahoma senate it is apparent that it is past the time for reform in the method of the selection of our state officials....

"This situation is also positive proof of the immediate necessity for judicial reforms if any doubt previously existed.

"As governor, I now call on all citizens and responsible organizations to join in cooperative action to bring about the future selection of judges on a non-partisan and non-political basis, in order that we may have the best informed, experienced and dedicated persons on our courts of justice and that these courts be completely free of political and partisan influence."[2]

The state's leading newspaper joined the chorus calling for court reform. The *Daily Oklahoman* editorialized, "JUDICIAL REFORM NEEDED NOW." "A better method of selecting the appellate and supreme court judges certainly is needed.... Too many high court officials are perpetuated in office through local or area political machines."[3]

The *Norman Transcript* wrote, "If any members of the Legislature need a clinching argument to convince them that Oklahoma's highest court system must be revised to insure against tampering with justices in the future, the conviction of O. A. Cargill, one of Oklahoma's most prominent attorneys, on a charge of perjury in connection with supreme court bribery cases, provides it in convincing fashion."[4]

"Do we want reform?" the *Oklahoma City Times* asked rhetorically. "...it must be obvious to all by now that we must do something about changing the method of selecting our judges... How can anyone be happy about the fact--now so vividly underlined--that a judge must depend for his re-election on campaign contributions from some of the very attorneys and firms who appear in his court?"[5]

The *Tulsa Tribune* stated the matter succinctly. "It's not a nickel's worth of good exposing supreme court bribery unless we then improve the system so scandals won't happen again."[6]

Nor had Oklahoma's travails escaped the notice of the national press. An April article in *Time Magazine* proclaimed, "Little in U.S. judicial history comes close to matching the scandal now swirling around the Oklahoma state supreme court." The article concluded, "Though it (the state bar association) cleared seven of the nine justices... the court has obviously suffered a crushing loss of prestige."[7]

More recently, an article in *Newsweek* magazine was headed "Cash-and-Carry Justice" and concerned the impeachment of Justice N. B. Johnson. It ended with a devastating comment: "Still the messy scandal wasn't at an end. Johnson and Welch still face trial on bribery charges, meaning Oklahomans will have to endure another round of gibes that the state has had the best justice money can buy."[8]

Once before, the state had attempted judicial reform. The previous November, a constitutional amendment, State Question 415, was on the ballot. This measure would have created a court of the judiciary, a group of judges with jurisdiction in cases involving removal from office and compulsory retirement of judges.

The measure failed by a narrow margin. Governor Bellmon attributed the loss to what he called the "silent vote." The irony is, the issue received more "yes" than "no" votes (397,823 vs. 370,694); however, it failed only because it didn't get an absolute majority of all ballots cast in the election (474,666 required for passage). This was the "silent vote" factor at work. That is to say, any person who failed to mark his ballot "yes" or "no" on this particular issue automatically had his ballot treated as being the equivalent of a "no."

Had S.Q. 415 passed in November, it could have saved the state a tremendous amount of shame and the agony in the impeachment trial.

When the 1965 legislative session opened under the cloud of

supreme court scandals, there was strong sentiment for it to take up the issue of judicial reform--particularly since S.Q. 415 had failed by such a narrow margin and only because of what many people considered a fluke. Confidence in the judiciary had been badly jolted in Oklahoma.

Of all the branches of popular government, the one that could least stand the taint of malfeasance was the one which sat in judgment on a person's property and money. Judge Samuel I. Rosenman, president of the New York Bar Association, said, "The elective system is the least likely of all methods to bring to judicial office the most qualified men."[9]

In only 15 states besides Oklahoma were judges elected in a partisan manner. Nineteen other states elected their judges on a non-partisan ballot. In the remaining 15 states, including neighboring Missouri, Kansas, Nebraska, and Iowa, judges were appointed by the governor with approval of the legislature. Reformers proposed that Oklahoma adopt a modified "Missouri Plan."

However, advocates of reform hadn't reckoned with an implacable foe in the person of House Speaker J. D. McCarty, who announced his opposition to any change in Oklahoma's system of electing judges by popular vote. The speaker described the proposed judge selection plan as "asinine and silly," despite the high praise it got from states in which the appointive method was used. McCarty claimed he would prefer the judgment of a million voters to that of a commission in the selection of judiciary officials.

Sarcastically, the *Enid Morning News* editorialized, "If McCarty is so sold on voter judgment, then why does he shun submission of these reforms, as constitutional amendments, to a public vote?" The editor goes on to ask, "Does he fear their adoption?" Finally, he concluded that McCarty's argument was weak and didn't hold water.[10]

Not withstanding the resistance of the legislature, the citizenry of Oklahoma was not standing still. Various efforts at reform were underway.

Governor Bellmon appointed an 18-member committee, chaired by Earl Sneed, dean of the University of Oklahoma Law School, to prepare recommendations for judicial reform. Sneed had long been an advocate of the "Missouri System," whereby supreme court justices are appointed by the governor and then are elected or rejected by the voters after a probationary period.

Sneed described Oklahoma's present system as "ancient, creaky, inefficient and outmoded," and said that pressure put upon judges to campaign is what concerns him most. "If a judge develops an effective campaign, it requires money," Sneed said. "Money given either to an aspiring or incumbent judge can create an obligation, or, even worse, constitute a direct or indirect bribe."[11]

In an interview given to a *Los Angeles Times* reporter, Sneed said it was questionable whether the Oklahoma legislature would vote to adopt an appointive system. He said, "Some of the biggest men in the legislature believe that everybody should be elected." This sentiment, he added, dates back to the days when populism was rife in Oklahoma and men believed all state officers had a right to be responsible to the people "and every man had a right to carry his appeal to the state's highest court."[12]

Less charitable than Sneed was Dale Cook, attorney for Governor Bellmon and former Assistant U.S. Attorney. Cook stated frankly, "The politicians don't like the idea of anybody being appointed. They see it as a threat to them."[13]

Another plan that saw little sign of approval was the "Oklahoma Plan" advocated by the Oklahoma Institute for Justice, a non-profit group comprised of a great many Oklahoma civic and community leaders, "laymen" as well as attorneys. Again, it was a modified "Missouri Plan" and consisted of three basic concepts:

1. nomination by a commission of a list of three qualified persons to fill each vacancy;

2. provisional appointment by the Governor of one of the three individuals so nominated; and

3. ratification at periodic intervals of the judge's tenure by the

voters.

The key to this plan was the nominating commission, which would be comprised of 13 persons elected as follows: six lay people, all elected by popular vote; six lawyers, elected by mail ballot from each of the congressional districts; and a chairman who would be selected by the Oklahoma Bar Association by mail ballot.[14]

Quietly at work in the background were some legislators also bent on reforms. Rep. Burke Mordy, Ardmore, introduced House Joint Resolution 523 which called for a procedure strikingly similar to that of the "Oklahoma Plan" of the Oklahoma Institute for Justice. The Mordy plan called for creation of a 13-member nominating commission, six lawyers elected by local bar associations in each congressional district, six lay persons elected by congressional districts, and a chairman elected by the state bar association.

Under the Mordy plan, the judge would serve six years before being ratified by the voters; under the Oklahoma Plan, the judge would serve 12 months before being ratified, then would go before the voters every six years thereafter. Under both plans, the ballot would contain the simple question, "Shall Judge ______________ be retained in office?"

Under the benign gaze of Speaker J. D. McCarty, house members shouted down the proposed judicial reform package on April 25, 1965. So confident were the foes of the "Mordy Plan" for selection of judges, they saw no point of going through the formality of a debate.

As it developed, their confidence was warranted. But the author of the measure, Rep. Mordy, insisted on defending the plan. The opposition didn't bother to present any counter argument. They had the votes.[15]

The senate, however, was not yet willing to give up on the possibility of reform, and it found a way to force a vote in the lower house. Senators Bryce Baggett and Cleeta John Rogers, both of Oklahoma City, piggybacked a reform amendment onto an existing house resolution (HJR 542) which was already intended to submit a proposed constitutional amendment to a vote of the people.

The Baggett-Rogers amendment provided that all judges, now elected, would serve out their terms unless removed for cause. As vacancies occurred on the supreme court and the court of criminal appeals, they would be filled by the governor from a list of three recommendations submitted by a non-partisan judicial nominating committee. As in the Mordy plan, the 13-member nominating commission would be comprised of six lawyers elected by the bar in each congressional district, six lay persons elected by voters of the district, and a chairman elected by the state bar association. Judges would serve six years, and at the end of their term would run on a non-partisan ballot labeled: "Shall (name of judge) be retained in office?"

McCarty called a news conference the next day, June 11, and bitterly assailed those who criticized him for helping to kill the previous plan, and he vowed to continue his sledgehammer attacks against the revived bill.

"I am unalterably opposed to taking the right to select judges away from the people which they have had since statehood," McCarty said. He said the senate plan revived on Thursday would not be buried in committee but would be hauled onto the house floor where he would "continue my opposition of this proposal, which was conceived in the minds of the corporations, large insurance companies, and others who think that a small group of intelligentsia has far greater wisdom than the voters of Oklahoma."[16]

On Tuesday, July 6, HJR 542, containing the reform package, came to a vote. On a voice vote, the house turned down the senate amendments which would call for a vote of the people on the new system for selecting judges.

Speaker McCarty was the key member against accepting the modifications. He aimed criticism at the bar association and said before he would favor giving the bar so many positions on a committee to recommend judges, the association "should come to the legislature with clean hands."

McCarty said the people pushing the appointment of judges were the ones advocating "one man, one vote" on legislative reapportionment. He said they now advocate "one man, no vote." He described Senators Bryce Baggett and Cleeta John Rogers, who proposed the amendment, as "those two phonies of the people."[17]

As a compromise measure, members of the house gratuitously passed a resolution introduced by Rep. James W. Connor which provided that the next session of the legislature (1967) shall in 90 days realign supreme court and courts of criminal appeals districts.

It was almost as if Oklahoma had invented corruption. Indeed, every time a national publication wrote an article about judicial corruption, it seemed as if they cited Oklahoma as "Exhibit A."

For example, in an August, 1966 article in the *Wall Street Journal* dealing with Americans' loss of confidence in their courts, the paper wrote: "The Oklahoma scandal seems to have had a profound impact. 'It just scares us all to death,' says a supreme court justice of another state here. 'I think it is one of the worst things that ever happened to the courts'."[18]

Commenting on this article, the editor of the *Oklahoma City Times* lamented, "The real tragedy is that, thanks to formidable roadblocks in the last legislature, we have done nothing in the way of reforms to redeem ourselves in the eyes of the nation."[19]

In the June 11, 1966, *The New Republic*, Oklahoma City attorney Burck Bailey wrote, "The villain in this sordid affair may be the method used in Oklahoma to fill judicial office.... The potential for corruption is inherent in the system. These payoffs, claimed Cargill and Corn, were simply 'campaign contributions'."[20]

Not to be outdone, the July, 1966 *Reader's Digest* published an article headed "Is That Judge Fit to Sit?" The article put forth the following egregious example:

"Three state supreme court justices in Oklahoma shared an alleged $150,000 bribe to 'throw' their decisions in favor of a shady investment company fighting a state tax claim. One justice has served a nine-month prison sentence for income-tax evasion; another has been convicted and impeached; the third has resigned under threat of impeachment."[21]

Again, the *Christian Science Monitor* took up the cudgel in a 13-part series. In the lead article on April 12, 1967, headed "A robe doesn't make a judge," correspondent Howard Jones wrote: "Even today some Oklahoma judges refuse to believe that members of their state supreme court took bribes, even though one has confessed and another is in prison." He added, "Some judges fear that a public airing of dirty judicial laundry will further reduce respect for law and order."[22]

When the 1967 session of the state legislature opened, it was without the leadership of J. D. McCarty. Occupying that post was Rep. Rex Privett. The three-term speaker and 26-year veteran of the house had been defeated in the November elections by GOP candidate Vondel L. Smith. Dewey Bartlett was now governor.

Almost immediately, the house took up the issue of judicial reform. On Wednesday, January 18, Rep. John McCune introduced the first of two judicial reform petitions. The first resolution called for a constitutional amendment that would reorganize the court system, doing away with justices of the peace and providing for district judges, associate district judges and special judges.

The second resolution, introduced a day later, would let people decide if they wanted to elect judges on a non-partisan basis; however, it would retain the elective system for all judges. Justices for the state's two highest courts would be elected by districts, but on a non-partisan ballot.[23]

Over on the other side of the Capitol, the senate was not satisfied with the lower chamber's proposal. Sen. Robert Gee, chairman of the senate judiciary committee, announced that they were going to come up with their own version of a court reform plan. In Gee's view, the house did not go far enough in the matter of taking politics out of the judicial selection process. The senate committee favored a plan that would call for the appointment of appellate judges.[24]

A month later, however, the senate reversed its own judiciary committee and put the non-partisan system of electing appellate judges back into the bill. Governor Bartlett, speaking that evening to about 100 persons at the annual Governor's Week at Oklahoma State University, deplored the action and urged the legislative conference committee to reinsert the elective process. He said he favored appointment of judges at the appellate level, which he felt was superior. "We are at the hoping point on this bill now," he said.

Meanwhile, the "Sneed Plan," favored by the League of Women Voters and other reform-minded groups, was still alive. It had been circulated as an initiative petition and gathered 142,377 signatures calling for a vote by the people. However, it was tied up in the Secretary of State's office because of challenges by protesting justices of the peace and some attorneys.

Supporters of the "Sneed Plan" were not giving up hope, however. Calling the plan the best proposed, backers had mailed over 3,000 letters of encouragement.[25]

Meanwhile, the old nemesis of reform, J. D. McCarty, was back in the headlines. In what might be considered a twist of ultimate irony, the deposed "king" of the Oklahoma House of Representatives, who had so heavy-handedly resisted reform in the courts, now found himself tangled in the very kind of scandal he had previously tried to protect. On April 7, 1965, he was indicted in federal court in Oklahoma City on charges of federal income tax evasion.

The six-count indictment returned by grand jury foreman Willis J. Wheat charged him with three counts of willful tax evasion and three counts of knowingly stating that his tax returns were accurate when he allegedly knew they were not.

Count one of the indictment stated that about May 29, 1961, McCarty and his wife filed a joint tax return for the year 1960,

But McCarty "Then and there well knew," the indictment stated, "that he had substantial additional income." Wording of the other counts was similar.[26]

A further ironic twist was revealed in the *Daily Oklahoman*. On a questionnaire filled out for the paper 14 years earlier, McCarty said he opposed enactment of a law requiring candidates for public office to make public their income tax returns. "I see no reason to single a candidate out," he said. "After all, their records are known among their neighbors and the community in which they live."[27]

The fight for an appointive system for appellate judges faced an uphill battle in the conference committee. Inasmuch as both houses of the legislature had already voted by majority for non-partisan election by districts, it would have been considered most unusual for the two houses to back up on their earlier position.

But miracles do happen. To most people's great surprise, on May 8 the house-senate conference committee approved a court reform package that gave people the opportunity to vote on an appointive-retentive process for judges on the supreme court and court of criminal appeals somewhat similar to the much-discussed Missouri Plan.

One factor cited for the surprising turnaround was a desire to head off the Sneed Plan which had now been cleared by the Secretary of State and was fighting its way through the supreme court. This plan, patterned on the model court plan proposed by the American Bar Association, was more heavily appointive and would give the legislature less power in controlling courts.

Statewide vote on the proposed constitutional amendments was set for July 11, 1967. To avoid confusing the voters, the two propositions were printed on different colored ballots.

State Question 448 was printed on a white ballot. It would streamline the courts by setting up a two-level system, with trial work being handled by district courts and appeals by the supreme court and the court of criminal appeals. The plan would also eliminate the justice of the peace courts, something many Oklahomans had long desired.

State Question 447, printed on a yellow ballot, would take the appellate courts out of politics by establishing an appointive-retentive system for selecting judges for the state's two highest courts. A vacancy would be filled by the governor from names submitted by a judicial nominating commission; and every six years the judge would run for re-election on his record. At the end of his or her term a judge would run on a separate ballot, without party designation, with the question: "Shall (name of judge) of (title of court) be retained in office?"

There was one further provision: The yellow ballot could not become operative unless the white ballot carried.

On Tuesday, July 11, 1965, with only a light voter turnout, Oklahoma's long, scandal-tarnished ordeal was over. Both constitutional amendments carried "Yes, yes."

The basic reform amendment (white ballot) carried 90,167 to 73,919, and the appointive-retentive amendment (yellow ballot) received 88,183 "yes" votes to 79,280 "no" votes.

Rep. John McCune, chief author of the basic reform plan, said "I am highly pleased that the people of Oklahoma have recognized the need for a new, modern streamlined court system."[28]

Sen. Robert Gee, chief advocate of the appointive-retentive system, commented, "I'm obviously very happy. I hope that all Oklahomans will join in now and assist the legislature in making this one of the finest judicial systems in the United States."[29]

Governor Bartlett was reached in Los Angeles on an industrial tour. He said, "I am very pleased that the Oklahoma voters have voted progressive changes in our court structure."[30]

The election commission had barely finished counting the ballots on court reform when an old campaigner found himself facing a new battle. Far from the smoky rooms and corridors of state government, long-time legislative leader J. D. McCarty stepped into the federal courtroom to hear Judge Luther Bohanon tap his gavel.

In one of the strange ways that history comes full circle, this was the same Luther Bohanon who, as an attorney nine years earlier, had exposed the missing $150,000 in the *Selected* case, and now he was about to write the final chapter on another tale of graft, greed and corruption.

Using similar accounting methods as those previously employed in the trial of Judge Welch, U.S. Attorney B. Andrew Potter demonstrated that McCarty spent more money than he reported as income. The difference was more than $32,000 for the years 1960-62, government accountants said. Included in the three-year total were $12,000 from the Oklahoma City Chamber of Commerce ''for help on bond issues and annexation programs'' and $5,000 from New Mexico racing interests.

In his defense, McCarty attributed the problem to bad bookkeeping rather than bad intentions. He said the girls in his office kept the books, and he was so busy with legislative duties that he didn't take time to check them carefully. McCarty also stated, ''At the capitol, nearly every other day people who had (insurance) policies with me and owed me would give me a check or cash.'' Some of this would be used as spending money, he said.

The case went to the jury shortly after noon on Saturday, July 22. At 9:10 p.m., after nearly nine hours of deliberation, the jury returned its verdict to Judge Bohanon. McCarty was found guilty on two of the six counts of income tax evasion.

McCarty paused a minute to smooth down his hair. He adjusted his suit jacket, took a deep breath, and walked out into the glare of television lights.

On September 16, McCarty was stunned by a three-year prison sentence which, after exhausting his appeals, he began serving November, 21, 1968. The old campaigner walked into prison with his head held high.[31] No one could say McCarty didn't go out in style: his conviction was tabbed by the Oklahoma Press

Association as the top news story of 1967.

After overcoming many legal hurdles, the long-delayed "Sneed Plan" finally was set for a vote of the people on September 17, 1968. By then, however, the reforms already established seemed to be doing their job, the image of the court was being restored, and voter interest seemed to be waning. In a light voter turnout, Oklahomans said "no" to the Sneed Plan by a count of 172,711 votes to 115,771, thus closing the door on further judicial reform.

14

Tainted Cases

There's an old saying around the courts that "A doctor buries his mistakes, a dentist can either fill in or pull out his mistakes, but the mistakes of a judge become the law of the land." Unfortunately, there is more than a kernel of truth to that.

One of the most disturbing things about the allegations against Oklahoma's Supreme Court justices was that it threw a cloud over the "case law" system. That is, if justices can be influenced or bribed, then all of the carefully constructed pyramid of legal precedent begins to crumble.

Case law means that any time a legal interpretation or judgment is made in one case, that becomes the law of the land and forms the basis for ruling all future cases dealing with similar issues. This means any time the supreme court makes a ruling--tainted or not--it becomes a part of the legal architecture. And if a ruling is tainted it means that all future decisions based on that ruling may be standing on very shaky ground.

Twenty-four years of bribe-taking confessed to by one ex-justice had created an enormous headache for the Oklahoma Supreme Court. Judge Corn's admission now threatened to open the floodgates to a torrent of appeals from disgruntled losers.

Fortunately, the U.S. Supreme Court did its part to head off the chaos which could have resulted from indiscriminate opening of opinions going back 24 years. It did this by refusing to hear a case in which the losers contended they were deprived of due process simply because an opinion adverse to their position was written by Justice N. B. Johnson, who was subsequently impeached for accepting bribes in another case--although they provided no evidence of bribery in their case.

This action by the U.S. high court made it clear that, good or bad, the pyramid of law built up by the Oklahoma Supreme Court in a quarter of a century of opinions would not be destroyed in one blow. It would require a case-by-case analysis and evidence of corruption.

The litany of wrongdoing included four former justices and a prominent attorney who, himself, once served temporarily as a special member of the court. These were:

* N. S. Corn, former justice who served a prison term for federal income tax evasion; admitted that he could not remember a year in 24 years on the court that he did not take a bribe.

* Earl Welch, former justice who served a prison term for federal income tax evasion; resigned from the court in 1965 under threat of impeachment.

* N. B. Johnson, former justice convicted and removed from office in 1965 by impeachment.

* Ben Arnold, former justice, now deceased, who had been accused of having "undue interest" in a case.

* O. A. Cargill, Sr., prominent attorney, convicted on federal perjury charges in connection with alleged bribery of state supreme court judges.

Now it was time for the court to clean up some unfinished business by going back and reviewing some of the tainted cases from the past. In three celebrated cases, the losers asked that old opinions be vacated on grounds of alleged bribery and other wrongdoing on the court.

Johnson v. Johnson

A petition to reopen the 1954 supreme court case was filed August 10, 1965. The case involved the estate of Dexter J. Johnson, a bachelor, who died in May, 1952, leaving an estate of more than $1.25 million.

After Dexter Johnson's death, a will was filed for probate in Oklahoma County court. This will, written on scratch paper, left his estate to Victor J. and Beulah J. Johnson, a brother and sister.

Another brother, Joseph E. Johnson filed a contest to the will, contending the will was not executed as required by state law.

Joseph E. Johnson's contention was upheld by both the county court and the district court, and was appealed to the supreme court. On December 15, 1952, the high court issued a unanimous opinion upholding the lower court ruling that the will was not legally drawn. A petition for rehearing was overruled in early 1954.

Although no application was filed for a second petition for rehearing, Justice Ben Arnold presented a motion in conference on February 15, 1954, to vacate the order. Then, on May 17, 1954, Arnold presented a substitute opinion for reversing the high court's previous opinion, which the court did on October 15, 1954, on a 5-to-4 vote. Concurring in the reversal opinion were Justices Arnold, Corn, Welch, Johnson, and Blackbird. Halley wrote a stinging dissent.

In their petition for the court to reopen the case, attorneys for the estate of Joseph Johnson contended that Corn was automatically disqualified from being a judge in the 1954 opinion by virtue of his having confessed to bribes in other cases.

A special supreme court was appointed to hear the petition, inasmuch as the five justices participating in the original decision who were still on the court--Halley, Jackson, Davison, Williams and Blackbird--had disqualified themselves. The case was reconsidered by five special judges named by the governor and four regular justices who had since been elected to the court.

On January 19, 1967, the court refused to vacate the opinion on grounds that Justice Corn took a bribe in another case. Otherwise, it said, such action would knock out more than 1,000 judgments of the past 26 years and create a "shambles." The question of law addressed by the court was, "Where a justice secretly agrees to take bribes from an individual and does not take them consistently, but such fact is unknown except to him and the bribe giver, does he thereby automatically become disqualified to participate in any further decision of this Court, so that his every vote thereafter is a nullity, even in cases where no wrongdoing occurred?" The court answered this question in the negative.

All was not lost, however. The court said it would reconsider its denial for a rehearing on the merits of the case if specific acts of wrongdoing could be shown.

Accordingly, attorneys for the Joseph Johnson estate filed a new plea to reopen the case. Their new brief cited the records of Corn, Welch and Johnson given in previous testimony, and they alleged that Arnold showed "undue interest" in the case. They also stated that Corn swore on July 13, 1965, that his vote "could have been caused" by orders from Cargill.

On June 27, 1968, the court handed down its decision. Petition to vacate the prior decision of the court was denied. The decision was unanimous.

In its opinion, the court wrote, "Although Arnold did recommend that the order denying the Petition for Rehearing be vacated and did submit a substitute opinion which was adopted, and there is evidence that 'he was just the power behind the discussion,' these facts do not reasonably establish to the satisfaction of this court that Arnold was *improperly* motivated."[1]

The court did not find that there was any irregularity in the procedure followed, and there was no evidence that O. A. Cargill was connected with or interested in the Johnson will case.

Further the opinion stated, "a former member of this Court testified that it isn't unusual for a Judge to fight for his opinion and what he thinks the law is, and that 'a Judge becomes or a Justice becomes an advocate for his views and, just like anyone, that is just the way the human mind operates'."[2]

Oklahoma Company v. O'Neil

Eugene O'Neil won a $120,000 oil lease lawsuit from the Oklahoma Company in county district court in Bartlesville, Oklahoma, April 25, 1957. The court held that a group of seven Florida and Massachusetts investors had been induced by fraud to invest $120,000 in an oil and gas lease, and as a result of this fraud they were entitled to get their money back.

The Oklahoma Co. was headed by Harold F. Westcott and Otha

Westcott, husband and wife, who were president and secretary, and the owners of all but one share of stock. Mrs. Westcott was the daughter of attorney O. A. Cargill, Sr.

Westcott appealed to the state supreme court. On December 2, 1958, the high court reversed the lower court and ruled in favor of the Oklahoma Co.

During the impeachment proceedings against Justice Johnson and again in the trial of O. A. Cargill, Sr., ex-Justice N. S. Corn testified that he received $7,500 from Cargill to throw the opinion in favor of the Oklahoma Co. The money was split three ways--$2,500 each for Corn, Welch and Johnson.

On the basis of Corn's testimony, O'Neil sought to reopen the case.

The first victory was achieved April 25, 1967, when the court vacated the 1958 decision on the grounds that it was not "constitutionally adopted." The court declared: "The case *(Oklahoma Co. v. O'Neil,* et al.) now stands at issue on the merits as if no opinion had ever been issued." This meant that the case would come before the court as if it were for the first time.

The court noted that the 1958 decision was decided by a bare 5 to 4 majority. If evidence showed that Corn's vote must be discounted because of the bribe, then the decision lost its 5-member majority, and thus was not a decision with only four in favor.

The Oklahoma Co. had argued that Cargill was not its attorney or its agent, and therefore such an act as alleged should not be held against the company. The court's opinion noted that fact, but added that "this court does not overlook the family relationship between the owners of the stock in the company and such attorney (Cargill)."[3]

The court also said it was unnecessary to determine if Cargill acted for the company, because if Corn did accept a bribe for his vote, then it could not be said that justice was administered "without sale."

Attorneys for the Oklahoma Co. had also attacked Corn's testimony on grounds that he had admitted he lied in some things, and "false in one thing, he is to be disbelieved in all things."

The high court observed that such a rule is not inflexible. "This court," it said, "may not ignore the confession and testimony of a former member... to the effect that he was offered and received a bribe for his vote in a case pending in this court."[4]

In its opinion, the court also distinguished between the Oklahoma Co. case and the Johnson will case which it had refused to open on the grounds that although Corn voted for it, he had not testified that he received a bribe for his vote.

Six members of the court (Jackson, Irwin, Davison, Williams, Blackbird, and myself) then disqualified ourselves from hearing the case when it came back up again, and, as is customary, Governor Dewey Bartlett named special judges to take our places.

On May 2, 1968, the special supreme court unanimously ruled to uphold the initial decision of the district court that a group of seven investors had been induced by fraud. By now, the original $120,000 settlement had grown with interest to an estimated $250,000 in value. Collecting it would be another problem; the Oklahoma Co. was by then out of business.

Marshall v. Amos

This was the third and last case in which the Oklahoma Supreme Court had been asked to invalidate old decisions on allegations of corruption.

H. D. Amos won a case in Cleveland County district court against H. G. and Ida B. Marshall, husband and wife, involving oil royalties with an estimated value of $150,000 to $200,000. The supreme court, in a 5-to-4 vote June 5, 1956, reversed the trial court and ruled in favor of the Marshalls.

The deciding vote in the 1956 opinion was cast by Justice N. S. Corn, who later testified that he was paid $4,000 in $100 bills by Oklahoma City attorney O. A. Cargill, Sr., to vote for the reversal.

On June 4, 1968, the supreme court knocked out the 12-year-old opinion. The ruling set the stage for the appeal to be heard anew on its merits.

The court wrote in its opinion: "We have examined the

admissible testimony of N. S. Corn and such testimony reasonably tends to establish to the satisfaction of this court that Corn did receive a bribe for his vote... Having set aside Corn's vote (in this case), said decision did not meet the requirements of...the Constitution of Oklahoma which provides that the concurrence of the majority (5 votes) of the supreme court shall be necessary to decide any question."[5]

The court concluded, "Having determined that the decision of this court, dated June 5, 1956, and styled *Marshall v. Amos*...was not constitutionally adopted, the mandate of this court issued therein is recalled and said decision is hereby vacated and set aside."[6]

Subsequently, on July 15, 1970, the court denied a petition for rehearing, and the case stood as originally decided in the county district court.

> Many forms of government have been tried in this world of sin and woe. No one pretends that democracy is perfect or all-wise. Indeed, it has been said that democracy is the worst form of government except all those other forms that have been tried from time to time.
>
> Winston Churchill
> *House of Commons*, Nov. 11, 1947

Author's Concluding Postscript

It has been thirty years since a bombshell landed on the Oklahoma judicial system. About that long ago the judicial system was reformed. All lawyers may not agree with the court's decisions, but to the knowledge of this writer there has been no rumor of corruption since then.

This does not mean the system is non-corruptible. I firmly believe, however, that it has taken a big step toward improvement. The weak spot in our system is that one judge can jeopardize a judicial system. In writing this, I believe there should be an awareness of the mistakes of the past. I believe a mistake, if looked upon correctly, can cause a person to be wiser.

I think the voters of this state should be more watchful of people in public office. Certainly the judges.

William A. Berry

Chapter Notes

Chapter 2

1. Weaver, Jace, *Then to the Rock Let Me Fly: Luther Bohanon and Judicial Activism* (Norman: University of Oklahoma Press, 1993), 52.

2. "Pierre Laval Led to Scandal," *Daily Oklahoman*, February 28, 1965, 14.

3. "Two Justices Post Bond on Tax Evasion Charges," *Oklahoma City Times*, April 9, 1964, 1.

4. "Corn Gets 18 months; Court Payoffs Charged," *Oklahoma City Times*, July 1, 1964, 1.

5. "High Court Justices Ask Corn to Resign at Once Following Tax Sentencing," *Daily Oklahoman*, July 2, 1964, 1.

6. *Ibid.*

7. "Bellmon Seeks Probe of 'Court Corruption'," *Daily Oklahoman*, July 2, 1964, 1.

8. "Government Says Money Not Held Prior to 1957," *Oklahoma Journal*, October 6, 1964, 1.

9. "Welch Spending Testimony Heard," *Tulsa Tribune*, October 7, 1964, 1.

10. "Welch Trial Told of Golden Jacket," *Daily Oklahoman*, October 8, 1964, 1.

11. "Corn Refuses to Answer Any Questions in Welch Trial," *Daily Oklahoman*, October 10, 1964, 1.

12. "Carroll Airs $150,000 Payoff to Justice Corn," *Oklahoma City Times*, October 12, 1964, 2.

13. "Welch Guilty of Tax Evasion," *Daily Oklahoman*, October 20, 1964, 1.

14. "Special Session on Welch Eyed," *Oklahoma Journal*, Oct. 21, 1964, 1.

15. "It's a Berry Boycott," *Oklahoma City Times*, January 4, 1965, 1.

Chapter 3

1. "Bellmon Seeks Probe of 'Court Corruption'," *Daily Oklahoman*, July 2, 1964, 1.

2. "Judge Faces Prison," *Daily Oklahoman*, July 2, 1964, 2.

3. "Bellmon Considering Special Session to Take up Welch Impeachment," *Daily Oklahoman*, October 21, 1964, 1.

4. "Welch Keeps Post Despite Guilty Ruling," *Oklahoma City Times*, October 20, 1964, 1.

5. *Oklahoma Bar Journal*, October 31, 1964, p. 1869.

6. "Welch Barred from Practicing Law by Supreme Court," *Daily Oklahoman*, December 11, 1964, 1.

7. *Ibid.*

8. *Ibid.*

9. "Welch Ouster Rules Drawn," *Oklahoma City Times*, January 4, 1965, 1.

10. "Welch Ouster Probe Asked," *Oklahoma City Times*, January 6, 1965, 1.

11. *House Journal*, January 6, 1965, 70.

12. "McCarty Likes First Week," *Oklahoma Journal*, January 8, 1965, 1.

13. "House Drags Welch Action, *Oklahoma City Times*, January 18, 1965, 1.

14. "Reprieve for Welch?" *Tulsa Tribune*, January 18, 1965, editorial.

15. *Oklahoma City Times*, January 18, 1965, *loc cit*.

16. *Ibid.*

17. "'King' J.D.'s Own Program Is Clicking," *Oklahoma City Times*, January 21, 1965, 1.

18. "Blankenship Tells 'Sordid, Sickening' Tale," *Oklahoma City Times*, January 21, 1965, 1.

19. "Bribery Tale 'Politics', Democrats Cry," *Oklahoma City Times*, January 21, 1965, 1.

20. *Ibid.*

21. "Blankenship Forces House Committee Inquiry Into Possible Bribery," *Daily Oklahoman*, January 22, 1965, 1.

22. *Ibid.*

23. *Ibid.*

Chapter 4

1. "Attacks On Court Rile Prosecutor," *Daily Oklahoman*, Feb. 5, 1965, 1.

2. "Yellow Belly Tag Gets Sharp Reply," *Oklahoma City Times*, February 5, 1965, 1.

3. *Ibid.*

4. "Cargill Indicted On 3 Perjury Counts," *Daily Oklahoman*, February 16, 1965, 1.

5. "Cargill Indicted by Jury," *Oklahoma Journal*, February 16, 1965, 1.

6. *Ibid.*

7. "Cargill Indicted On 3 Perjury Counts," *Daily Oklahoman*, February 16, 1965, 1.

8. "Is O. A. Cargill 'Mr. X'?" *Oklahoma Journal*, February 16, 1965, 1.

9. "O. A. Cargill Perjury Trial Expected by April 1," *Oklahoma City Times*, February 16, 1965, 1.

10. "Potter Warns Against 'Pre-Trial Revelation'," *Oklahoma Journal*, February 16, 1965, 1.

11. "No Excuse For Waiting," *Oklahoma City Times*, February 24, 1965, editorial.

12. "Justice Denies Any Bribery Knowledge," *Oklahoma City Times*, February 24, 1965, 1.

13. "Earl Welch Still Writing Rulings," *Oklahoma City Times*, March 2, 1965, 1.

14. "Probers Told Judge Welch Still Working," *Paul's Valley Democrat*, March 2, 1965.

15. "Earl Welch Still Writing Rulings," *Oklahoma City Times*, March 2, 1965, 1.

16. "Judges Say Welch Still Getting Cases," *Daily Oklahoman*, March 3, 1965.

17. "Jury To Investigate High Court Activity Over Past 25 Years," *Daily Oklahoman*, February 23, 1965, 1.

18. "Another Supreme Court Fix Claim Unveiled To Probers," *Oklahoma City Times*, March 3, 1965, 1.

19. *Ibid.*

20. *Ibid.*

21. "Justice Fought For 'Selected'," *Oklahoma City Times*, March 3, 1965, 1

22. *Ibid.*

23. *Ibid.*

Chapter 5

1. "Johnson Asked To Take Lie Test, Withholds Answer," *Oklahoma City Times*, March 9, 1965, 1.

2. "Justice Johnson Given Deadline on Lie Detector Test," *Daily Oklahoman*, March 10, 1965, 7.

3. *Ibid.*

4. *Oklahoma City Times*, March 9, 1965, *Loc. Cit.*

5. *Ibid.*

6. *Daily Oklahoman*, March 10, 1965, *Loc. Cit.*

7. "Welch Skirts Lie Test Query By Investigators," *Oklahoma City Times*, March 10, 1965, 1.

8. *Ibid.*

9. *Ibid.*

10. *Ibid.*

11. *Ibid.*

12. *Ibid.*

13. "No Deals, Welch Told By Probers," *Oklahoma Journal*, March 11, 1965, 1.

14. "Lie Test Refused By Johnson," *Oklahoma City Times*, Mar. 11, 1965, 1.

15. "Welch Swayed Johnson, Aide Claims," *Daily Oklahoman*, March 17, 1965.

16. *Ibid.*

17. "Corn Reaffirms Statement Of Court Payoff," *Oklahoma Journal*, March 17, 1965, 1.

18. "Most Of Suit Cash Vanishes, Probers Told," *Oklahoma City Times*, March 16, 1965, 1.

19. "Probers Show Vote 'Pattern' In High Court," *Oklahoma City Times*, March 17, 1965, 1.

20. *Ibid.*

21. *Ibid.*

22. "Cargill Refuses To Talk At Quiz," *Daily Oklahoman*, Mar. 19, 1965, 1.

23. *Ibid.*

24. "Text Of Welch's Letter," *Tulsa Tribune*, March 22, 1965, 1.

25. "Corn Is Key Figure In Impeachment Trial," *Oklahoma City Times*, March 25, 1965, 1.

26. *Ibid.*

27. "Confusion Clouding Impeachment Move: Evidence of Bribe Disputed," *Oklahoma City Times*, March 24, 1965, 1.

28. *Ibid.*

Chapter 6

1. "To Improve the High Court," *Tulsa Tribune*, July 7, 1965, editorial.

2. *Ibid.*

3. "$25,000 Bribe Offer Bared By High Court Justice," *Oklahoma City Times*, March 11, 1965, 1.

4. "Judges Back N. B. Johnson," *Oklahoma City Times*, March 4, 1965, 1.

5. Editorial, *North Star*, June 19, 1958.

6. "Former Attorney Harlan Grimes Also Testifies," *Oklahoma City Times*, February 25, 1965.

Chapter 7

1. "Welch Resigns State High Court Post; Justice Johnson Is Facing Impeachment," *Tulsa Tribune*, March 22, 1965, 1.

2. "Accused Justice's Record Tops," *Oklahoma City Times*, January 21, 1965, 3.

3. "Welch, Johnson, Cargill Hit By Bribery Charges," *Tulsa Tribune*, March 27, 1965, 1.

4. *Ibid.*

5. "Senators Call For Johnson's Plea Monday," *Daily Oklahoman*, April 7, 1965, p. 1.

6. *Ibid.*

7. "Johnson Hires Two Attorneys," *Daily Oklahoman*, April 9, 1965, 1.

8. "Johnson Impeachment Trial Scheduled May 6," *Oklahoma Journal*, April 13, 1965, 1.

9. *Ibid.*

10. "Johnson Wins Opening Round of Ouster Trial," *Oklahoma City Times*, May 6, 1965, 1.

11. *Transcript*, 55.

12. *Transcript*, 59.

13. *Transcript*, 74.

14. *Transcript*, 75.

Chapter 8

1. "Former Colleagues Face Off In Scandal-Scourged Trial," *Tulsa Tribune*, May 7, 1965, 1.

2. *Transcript*, 80-81.

2. *Transcript*, 82.

4. *Transcript*, 83.

5. *Transcript*, 85.

6. *Transcript*, 91.

7. "Stern Justice Corn Won't Be Stampeded," *Oklahoma City Times*, May 7, 1965, 1.

8. *Ibid.*

9. *Transcript*, 98.

10. *Transcript*, 102-103.

11. *Transcript*, 107.

12. *Transcript*, 113.

13. *Transcript*, 113.

14. *Transcript*, 119.

15. *Transcript*, 111.

16. *Transcript*, 132.

Chapter 9

1. *Transcript*, 167-168.

2. *Transcript*, 189.

3. *Transcript*, 190.

4. "Court Podiums Stir Comment By Lawyers," *Oklahoma City Times*, May 8, 1965, 2.

5. *Transcript*, 251.

6. *Transcript*, 254.

7. *Transcript*, 272.

8. *Transcript*, 297.

9. *Transcript*, 297.

10. *Transcript*, 300.

11. *Oklahoma City Times*, May 11, 1965.

12. *Transcript*, 301.

13. "Anti-Indian Bias Hinted by Judge," *New York Times*, May 12, 1965.

14. "Johnson Defense Suffers Setback," *Tulsa Tribune*, May 12, 1965, 1.

15. "Jury Restless as Trial's End Nears," *Oklahoma City Times*, May 13, 1965, 1.

16. "Johnson Asks for Acquittal; Court 'Clean-Up' Demanded," *Oklahoma City Times*, May 13, 1965, 1.

17. "Senate Finds Justice Johnson Guilty of Two Bribery Charges," *Daily Oklahoman*, May 14, 1965, 2.

18. Personal interview with author, June 11, 1992.

19. "Johnson Found Guilty," *Oklahoma Journal*, May 14, 1965, 1.

Chapter 10

1. *Plutarch's Lives*, Caesar, sec 10: "Caesar's wife must be above suspicion."
2. Aristotle, *Ethics*, Book III, Ch. 1.
3. *Model Code*, Canon 3A(4).
4. *Model Code*, Canon 5C(1)
5. *Harrison v. Barton*, No. 39414.
6. *Application of Oklahoma Turnpike Authority*, No. 39359.
7. *Hoover et al v. Riesen et al*, No. 39975.

Chapter 11

1. "Cargill Case Judge Likes Cigars, Jurors," *Oklahoma Journal*, June 1, 1965.
2. "Judge Reveals Cargill Jury Switched Just Before Trial," *Oklahoma Journal*, June 22, 1965, 1.
3. "O. A. Cargill Perjury Trial Expected by April 1," *Oklahoma City Times*, February 16, 1965, 1.
4. "Justice Has Seizure, Cargill Lawyer Claims," *Oklahoma City Times*, June 1, 1965, 1.
5. *Ibid.*
6. "Cargill Trial Jury Picked, Locked Up," *Oklahoma Journal*, June 2, 1965, 2.
7. "Carroll Says Cargill Invented 'Laval' Story," *Oklahoma Journal*, June 3, 1965, 2.
8. "Pierre Laval Story Invented by Cargill, Carroll Says at Trial," *Daily Oklahoman*, June 3, 1965, 2.
9. "Cargill Trial to Last at Least Two Weeks?" *Oklahoma City Times*, June 3, 1965, 1.
10. "Carroll Bares His Decision to Tell Truth on 'Payoffs'," *Tulsa Tribune*, June 3, 1965, 4.
11. "Three Other Justices Enter Corn Testimony," *Tulsa Tribune*, June 4, 1965, 1.
12. *Ibid.*
13. "Justices Deny Any Bribery," *Oklahoma Journal*, June 5, 1965, p. 2.
14. "Three Other Justices Enter Corn Testimony," *Tulsa Tribune*, June 4, 1965, 4.
15. *Ibid.*
16. *Ibid.*
17. "Cargill Made Deals With Rival Lawyers, Former Justice Says," *Daily Oklahoman*, June 5, 1965, 2.
18. "Corn's Gambling Role Probed; Trip Recalled," *Oklahoma City Times*, June 7, 1965, 2.

19. "Bid to Hire Cargill Aired," *Oklahoma City Times*, June 8, 1965, 2.

20. "Words Fly; Miskovsky Quits," *Oklahoma Journal*, June 12, 1965, 1.

21. "Witness Tells Court Reversal Cost $50,000," *Oklahoma Journal*, June 9, 1965, 2.

22. *Ibid.*

23. "Cargill Judge, Lawyer Clash (Over Witness)," *Oklahoma City Times*, June 10, 1965, 2.

Chapter 12

1. "Witness Says Bayless Got Big Fee in Marshall Case," *Tulsa Tribune*, June 12, 1965, 1.

2. *Ibid.*

3. "Cargill Jurors Told of $150,000 Cache Buried Under Water," *Daily Oklahoman*, June 11, 1965, 2.

4. *Ibid.*

5. "Six Justices Deny Any Deal With Cargill," *Tulsa Tribune*, June 11, 1965, 4.

6. *Ibid.*

7. "Cargill's Perjury Case Nears Jury," *Daily Oklahoman*, June 12, 1965, 2.

8. *Ibid.*

9. *Ibid.*

10. "Confusion Rattles Cargill Defense," *Oklahoma City Times*, June 12, 1965, 1.

11. "Cargill Denies Bribes From Witness Stand," *Sunday Oklahoman*, June 13, 1965, 2.

12. "Cargill Closes Defense, Denies Bribery," *Oklahoma City Times*, 1.

13. *Ibid*, 2.

14. "Nance Bares Cargill Bribe Offer," *Oklahoma Journal*, June 15, 1965, 1.

15. *Ibid.*

Chapter 13

1. "Cargill 'Victim of Enemies'; Prosecutor Cries 'Bribery!'" *Oklahoma City Times*, June 15,1965, 1.

2. "Governor Urges Speedy Reforms," *Daily Oklahoman*, May 14, 1965, 1.

3. "Judicial Reform Needed Now," *Daily Oklahoman*, May 7, 1975, editorial.

4. "Cargill Verdict Aids Reform Plan," *Norman Transcript*, June 16, 1965, editorial.

5. "Do We Want Reform?" *Oklahoma City Times*, June 9, 1965, editorial.

6. "What Dare They Do?" *Tulsa Tribune*, June 28, 1965, editorial.

7. "Judges: Oklahoma's Shocking Scandal," *Time Magazine*, April 16, 1965, 47.

8. "Oklahoma: Cash and Carry Justice," *Newsweek*, May 24, 1965, 37-38.

9. "For Better Judges," *Tulsa Tribune*, January 31, 1965, editorial.

10. "Judicial Reforms Dying Slow Death," *Enid Morning Sun*, repeated in *Daily Oklahoman*, June 20, 1965, editorial.

11. "Court Scandal Taxes State Pride," *Oklahoma Journal*, May 25, 1965, 1.

12. *Ibid.*

13. *Ibid.*

14. *Oklahoma Institute for Justice*, May 1965, pp. 1-3.

15. "House Casually Kills Missouri Plan," *Tulsa Tribune*, April 29, 1965, 3.

16. "McCarty Vows Battle Against Court Plan," *Tulsa Tribune*, June 11, 1965, 2.

17. "House Says 'No' to Judicial Plan," *Daily Oklahoman*, July 7, 1965, 3.

18. "Courts Crisis: Oklahoma Always Cited," *Wall Street Journal*, reprinted in *Oklahoma City Times*, August 19, 1965, editorial page.

19. "Our Scandal Cited," *Oklahoma City Times*, August 19, 1965, 42.

20. Burck Bailey, *The New Republic*, June 11, 1966, 8-9.

21. *Reader's Digest*, July 1966, 127-131.

22. "A Robe Doesn't Make a Judge," *Christian Science Monitor*, April 12, 1967, Section 2, 1.

23. "Reform Move In Committee," *Daily Oklahoman*, January 19, 1967, 4.

24. "Senators Rush Court Reform Plan of Own," *Daily Oklahoman*, March 29, 1967, 3.

25. "'Sneed Plan' Ballot Drive to Continue," *Daily Oklahoman*, February 26, 1967, 4.

26. "Tax Indictment Names McCarty," *Daily Oklahoman*, April 7, 1967, 1.

27. *Ibid.*

28. "Both Court Questions Carry: Turnout Light As Issues Get Small Margin," *Daily Oklahoman*, July 12, 1967, 1.

29. *Ibid.*

30. *Ibid.*

31. "J.D. Prison-Bound, Head High," *Daily Oklahoman*, Nov. 21, 1968, 1.

Chapter 14

1. *Johnson v. Johnson*, No. 39937.

2. *Ibid.*

3. *Oklahoma Co. v. O'Neil*, No. 38178.

4. *Ibid.*

5. *Marshall v. Amos*, No. 36936.

6. *Ibid.*

Index